In Praise of Goodness

IN PRAISE OF GOODNESS

GOD'S DREAM

LYNN CRINER

Copyright Lynn Criner © 2025

All rights reserved. No part of this book may be reproduced,
stored in a retrieval system, or transmitted in any form or by any means—
electronic, mechanical, photocopy, recording, or any other—
except in the case of brief quotations embodied in critical articles
and reviews, without the prior permission of the publisher.

Printed and Distributed by HSA Publications

Cover design and text layout by Jonathan Gullery

ISBN Paperback 978-1-931166-45-4

Cover Photo: Reverend Sun Myung Moon and Dr. Hak Ja Han Moon
Frontispiece Photo: Reverend Sun Myung Moon
and Dr. Hak Ja Han Moon at Cheongpyeong Lake, South Korea

Printed in the United States of America

CONTENTS

Part One: My Journey

My Roots 5
Folk Music and the Civil Rights Movement 9
An Unexpected Transformation 15
Lifegiving Lectures 21
Jesus Calls Sun Myung Moon 27
A Great Price 31
Deepening My Religious Life 37
Rev. Sudo's Injured Shoulder 41
Meeting the Lord Jesus 45
God Dwelling in the Family 49
Salvation Through the Marriage Blessing 53
Suggesting a Spouse 59
A Difficult Mission 63
Early Days with Mrs. Moon 67
Peace on Earth 71
Communism and the Free World 79

Part Two: Sharing Life With Rev. And Mrs. Moon

Personal Experiences with Rev. Moon 89
Pastor in Idaho 93

That Everyone May Eat	97
I Go Fishing with Rev. Moon	101
Rev. Moon's Second Son	107
A Good Life	111
A Good Community	115
Persecution	119
Rev. Moon Ascends to the Spiritual World and Comforts Me	125
Mother of Peace	129
Cheongpyeong Holy Ground	137

Part Three:
Reflections On God's Providence

Spiritual Growth	143
Internal Selflessness and Absolute Purity	147
Eternal Respect	151
Messages for the Heart	155

Part Four: Essays

Christianity's Gift of Freedom to America	163
Becoming a Better Teacher	173

PART ONE

My Journey

I have led an unexpectedly good life, actually an amazing life, but the marvelous and fulfilling things I've experienced didn't happen because I was adventurously taking chances. Throughout my early adult life, I was quietly searching for clearer understanding, for deeper, more comprehensive truth.

In those years, I lived with an almost unconscious sense that there was a higher, freer world out there somewhere. At the same time, like other people of my generation – or perhaps any generation – I wrestled with thorny questions: Why does evil persist unabated despite our best efforts to overcome it? Why does history move in unexpected and unpredictable ways? Why isn't there more kindness in the world?

My parents were both college professors, and I felt well acquainted with the intellectual world around me. I wasn't expecting to find a thinker who could help me in any significant way, but I did.

I met a teacher who surprised me by shedding light on the larger questions about the human condition that generally remain unanswered. This teacher, who turned out, unexpectedly, to be the Lord of the Second Advent, was the doorway to the wonderful things that happened in my life, but I should start at the beginning.

My Roots

My family was well connected intellectually and artistically, so well connected, in fact, that I didn't actually have a lot of hope that I would encounter anyone who could deal with the issues hovering in the back of my mind. My dad's successful associates inclined me to suppose that realistically it might not be possible for me, or anyone, for that matter, to find the kind of truth I was seeking.

My dad knew celebrated creative people. The writer F. Scott Fitzgerald was among his friends. Fitzgerald invited my father to come with him when he moved from Baltimore to New York City. Together they took in the New York literary scene, enjoying life. I remember my dad telling me about one late night when they got a taxi and rode down 5th Ave. with Fitzgerald riding on top of the cab looking at the stars.

My father had enrolled in Johns Hopkins University when he was sixteen and the same year had started working at Baltimore's daily newspaper, the *Baltimore Sun*. Later, he received a Nieman Fellowship at Harvard, an award given to outstanding journalists. Following his time at Harvard, he became a professor teaching journalism at the University of Massachusetts.

I grew up listening to my father talking for long hours with journalists who were his friends: Charlie Morton, editor of the *Atlantic Monthly*; A.D. Emmart, editor of the *Baltimore Sun*; Herman Dinsmore, editor of the international edition of the *New York Times*; T.S. Matthews, editor of *Time* magazine.

These journalists were thoughtful, interesting men with wide-ranging knowledge and well-informed judgment. Their conversations were anchored in their sense of the world as a whole and the role of America in that world, not just the news of the day or latest "gotcha" scoop that exposed wrongdoing.

My mother was curious about the nature of language. She first discovered the philosophy of language and then moved on to experimental psychology, designing experiments that probed how people learn language. Eventually she became head of the Psychology Department at Smith College.

My Roots

My parents were imaginative, fun, well-informed, creative, honest, flexible, optimistic, curious, gentle. Both of them shaped my life, but I especially remember my mother talking with me one night. She came into my room as I was doing my high school homework. I don't know what prompted her thoughts, but she said, "You know, Lynn, there are people literally dying because they're unable to find meaning in their lives. Please study and maybe you'll have some ideas that would help them." This thought was encouraging.

I went to college early and studied summer and winter, majoring in political history and political philosophy. I planned to become a college professor like my parents. As I neared graduation, I was at the top of my class and had already taken some of the graduate level courses, but privately I was aware that my understanding of two central issues in my discipline wasn't adequate.

I was nineteen, and at the time, I couldn't account for the contrast between the Marxists' vision of the good life and the heart-stopping, mind-boggling, unbelievably appalling amount of communist killing that had followed communist victories. I was aware that literally tens of millions of civilians in communist countries around the world – farmers, workers in all the trades, shop keepers, students, teachers, and other ordinary people — had perished inside these countries as communists sought to "eliminate obstacles" to their imagined utopia.

I could understand that communist killing was the result of an unrealistic hope unfulfilled. I could understand that theoretically. What I couldn't grasp was what it is in human nature that allows human beings to be that brutal.[1]

I was also perplexed by my logical positivist professor's claim that value judgments cannot be verified. I trusted my values, generally speaking, but I needed to think more carefully about how to defend them.

---

1 Here is an example of a heartless communist policy: When Stalin decided to collectivize the farms in Ukraine, his plan was rejected by the Ukrainian farm owners. Stalin responded by removing all the food he could find in Ukraine. Millions of Ukrainians starved to death – possibly as many as ten million. The worldwide total of communist killings dwarfs the Holocaust, though the underlying mystery of how people can be so ruthless is essentially the same. Those readers interested in knowing more about communism's dismal human rights record can read the books of Robert Conquest, Aleksandr Solzhenitsyn, Yang Jisheng, and other authors.

Folk Music and the Civil Rights Movement

I decided to take a year off before graduate school to study on my own. It was 1962. I went to Boston and was invited to edit Boston's folk music newspaper, *Boston Broadside*. I enjoyed Boston's small community of folk musicians and song writers.

Folk music gained widespread popularity after the Newport Folk Festival in the summer of 1963. The following fall, the folk music critic for the *New York Times*, Robert Shelton, asked me to work with him to package a national folk music magazine, *Hootenanny*. It was a pleasant job. I wasn't closer to resolving the intellectual issues I cared about. The books I was reading at the time didn't give me the insights I needed, but I was learning other things.

I had grown up in a secular humanist home that was not unfriendly to religion. My father had a private interest in both Christianity and Buddhism. Still, the concept of a purposeless universe was contemplated in our household as well.

The folk music I listened to night after night was filled instead with religious imagery and moral wisdom expressed beautifully in poetry that remained in my heart — songs like "All Come Angel Band." Still, I had no clearer sense of how anyone could know with any certainty that God existed or that morality had a firm foundation.

The musicians in my life were active in the civil rights movement, and I was committed to it, too. I saved money to go to Mississippi for Mississippi Freedom Summer in 1964. Though it was pretty clear to me at the outset that not all the people who travelled to Mississippi were going to live to return, I was willing to take a risk for a good cause.

When I went to apply, to my surprise I was told that while the original invitation had been for half the summer or the whole summer, there were already enough volunteers who could go for the whole summer. I didn't have enough money or time off to go for the whole summer. I wasn't needed.

A few months earlier, I had been fortunate enough to travel to Atlanta to join civil rights organizers from all over the South meeting in an African-American seminary. We sang much of the time we were together. People talked about the things that inspired them and shared their organizing techniques, their experiences, their prayers.

The Georgia Sea Island Singers were in Atlanta with us, too, singing music that had been handed down since the days of slavery. Their music touched me as almost nothing else ever has. The way they sang and moved together was a testimony to spiritual lives shaped by a day-after-day experience of powerlessness, of wishing to reach out to help other people who were beyond the singers' ability to protect. Songs sung from the soul were all that could be given. The atmosphere this music created had a rare depth that was close to the hearts of the civil right organizers. They, too, were in danger of losing their lives, and they cared about others they might not be able to protect.

Since the civil rights movement was born out of the African-American churches, most of the music we sang was religious music. "Up over my head, I see freedom in the air. You know I really do believe there is a God somewhere." These songs stayed with me though I was simply trying to be true to my ethical principles.

I respect nonviolence as a way of demonstrating the

moral value of loving one's enemies. Loving one's enemies is one of the great universal ideals, and, of course, it is central to Christianity. I'm aware that war is sometimes unavoidable, but loving one's enemies remains a way of life worth striving for. This belief drew me to Rev. Dr. Martin Luther King, Jr. and later to the Lord of the Second Advent, who educated me so richly.

Among the African-Americans I met in the civil rights movement were some of the finest people I've ever known. I felt and still feel that the nonviolent civil rights movement held the moral high ground. Thus, it was a hard lesson for me when the movement began to fall apart after making progress, but not enough. The admirable moral character of so many anonymous people in that movement was not going to be as widely appreciated as I knew it should be, and racism still lurked.

People have various opinions about the decline of the civil rights movement. I won't revisit the complex story here beyond reviewing a few of the well-known trends and events that brought it to a halt: the assassination of Rev. Dr. Martin Luther King, Jr.; communist aggression in Vietnam against which non-violence was powerless; the rise of the Black Panthers with their embrace of guns over non-violence which created a different image of African-Americans in the public's mind; and the occasional outbursts of vandalism by frustrated African-American teenagers, which didn't help. Whatever the particular causes, it is hard to express the exceedingly painful personal awareness I had of the interplay between good and evil in which the world is caught, a reality that is so often beyond our control.

Some of the folk musicians I knew believed that if we could just overcome racism and everybody could be paid a living wage, the world would be a good world. I hoped for these things but doubted that kind of progress alone would eradicate evil. History is too complex. Beyond folk music and the civil rights movement, there were things I still wanted to know about human nature that nobody around me seemed to be talking about.

Soon the Beatles and other British bands came to America. I worked for a year at a magazine that covered them, but I was ready to move on. Fortunately, I was able to join a small press with staff members who were writing a book on Nazi Germany. I learned quite a bit about Nazi Germany, though my deeper questions about the capacity for evil in the human heart remained. If anything, the more I delved into the history of evil, the larger the questions loomed.

What was at the root of the almost unimaginable evil that seemed to crop up from time to time, or that persisted for centuries essentially unopposed as in the case of Africans sold into slavery for five hundred years?

Eventually, I became involved in the theater in New York City and decided to teach school in Harlem. I had edited text long enough that I needed to spend more time around people, and I like kids. I hoped African-Americans could have higher incomes so I wanted them to have good educations. The kids in my class were imaginative and interesting. Every one of my third-graders could paint beautiful abstract paintings.

I supervised an after-school group whose parents were working 9-to-5, so their children couldn't go home at 3:00 o'clock. I started the Peace and Butter Restaurant in one corner of my room where the after-school kids could cook pancakes and hotdogs. All the children could cook safely and competently, but not all of them could read well enough. Some of them needed quite a bit of help, sometimes more than I could give. I still mentally divide students into two groups based on whether or not they can get help at home. Too many who can't need tutors.

An Unexpected Transformation

I had been teaching school for about eight months when one evening, to my astonishment, my underlying worldview was abruptly and dramatically transformed. I was friends with a playwright and poet named Grandon Conover. One evening as we were walking down the street in Greenwich Village, he asked, "Lynn, do you believe in God?" If anyone else had asked, I likely would have said, "No." I still had no idea how people could justify such a belief.

This friend was the only person I've known who was so raw in his pursuit of truth that he seemed willing to risk even his sanity so you could speak truthfully. To my surprise, as I paused trying to answer with deeper honesty, I had a spiritual experience. Please don't imagine we were using drugs. We didn't use drugs, and we weren't drinking.

Standing there on the sidewalk in the evening twilight, I felt my spirit moving up through a spiritual realm toward ever higher dimensions. I had a sense that God was there beyond that spiritual world. God seemed so far away that I couldn't say that I actually knew anything about God.

But, "Yes," I replied.

"You mean you really believe there's a spiritual being there who isn't just another human being. You think God is there?"

"Yes," I said simply.

I didn't tell my friend about my spiritual experience because I was still trying to digest it. I've come to believe that similar spiritual experiences have been shared across the ages by people of various faiths, but at that moment, I couldn't talk about what had just happened. It was too private and outside of my usual state of mind.

My spiritual experience unconsciously reminded me of another simpler religious experience – one I had in high school when I was often a soloist in the local churches. At a peaceful Easter sunrise service as I had seen the early light coming through stained-glass windows, I had almost felt for a moment that God was present in the natural world stretching beyond those windows. I had brushed the thought aside having no means to pursue it.

My friend the playwright, it turned out, believed that God lived at St. Patrick's Cathedral. Grandon wasn't Catholic or even exactly Christian, but St. Patrick's belongs to New York City in a sense. He went there to meditate and gain clarity. Later, after he had died, I went there, too.

My spiritual experience had solidified my awareness that God is real, but I felt I might never know anything concrete about God because God seemed so far away.

I went on with my life as it was. I finished the school year.

Then the following summer, my life changed again. I was injured in an accident. I was visiting my parents when it turned out that friends needed help moving a sofa. I picked up one end, and as we moved the sofa, it came crashing down on me. After that, my backbone protruded — I looked distinctly like a stegosaurus. Had my back been injured a bit more, I might have been paralyzed.

I rested on my parents' floor while slowly recovering. Lying on the floor, I had a second spiritual experience. I felt a pure, transcendent consciousness near me. I grasped then that God is aware of and cares about all the things that happen to everyone everywhere in the world.

That was my first understanding of God's nature — that God cares about the things that happen to us, that God's heart is the heart of a concerned parent. My understanding obviously wasn't novel as it is central to Christianity.

After that, I wanted to know about God more than I wanted anything else – unconsciously probably even more than I cared about staying alive though I wasn't taking chances. When my back was partially healed and protected by a back brace, I returned to New York City. Too injured to teach school, I did temporary office work.

Meanwhile, I searched for God everywhere ... in the sunsets that shone under elevated subway tracks in the Bronx, in the restaurants full of noisy people, in the animated conversations among my mostly Jewish neighbors, in the signs in front of miscellaneous churches and synagogues. My search went on for a little more than seven months.

Then, late one night I had yet another mystical experience. I was lying on the floor as I did every night after my back injury, when for the first time, I felt God's higher realm of love surrounding me. I could feel that heaven is filled with God's sensitive heart and is inspiringly beautiful. In that moment, God's love was so personal. Nobody, not even my beloved family, had loved me that deeply or known me that well.

The following night I had still another spiritual experience. This time, in a moment that touched my heart, I felt that God was satisfied that I clearly know that God and heaven are real. Since I am only one person, it seemed almost impossible that God would care, but it felt true.

After these spiritual experiences, following the path of my friend the playwright, I went to St. Patrick's Cathedral and sat in the pews. A Mass was being said. In that echoing solemnity, I asked God, "Does this have anything to do with You?"

"Yes," came the spiritual reply.

This opened my eyes more clearly to the value of Christianity, but I still kept to myself. I was in a private world and wanted to explore my life with God internally. I was familiar with Christian beliefs from the time I had spent singing in churches, and even more deeply from the civil rights movement. I try to abide by Christianity's moral principles, but I hadn't found the knowledge yet that fully answered my questions.

Lifegiving Lectures

The day before Christmas in 1974, I was making a delivery for my office. I got to the corner of 5th Ave. and 42nd St. near the New York Public Library. There on the corner stood a Japanese woman in her late twenties or early thirties.

"Would you like to go to a lecture?" she said softly, handing me a flyer. It turned out she was referring to a series of lectures being given that afternoon by several lecturers.

I like lectures. "Sure," I said, "but I have to make a delivery. I'll come back." When I got back, I had missed the first one. The Japanese woman hesitated but ushered me in to hear the second.

The second lecture was on the nature and origin of evil, and it was so profound, so broad, so nuanced that

I continue to find it useful in thinking about an enormous amount of human experience. It shed light on topics ranging from my thoughts about my own character, to things that happen in human relationships, to politics and the sweep of world history. All the lectures given that afternoon by this well-educated, highly articulate group of lecturers were valuable. They were teaching the thought of a remarkable man.

Suddenly I had encountered the wisdom of a thinker who knew things I wanted to know. This person, to my surprise, turned out to be Rev. Sun Myung Moon from Korea.

I was vaguely aware of him. A few months earlier he had given a free talk in Madison Square Garden. New York City had been plastered with posters for this event proclaiming that "September 18th Could Be Your Rebirthday." Rev. Moon's picture was on the posters. Like so many New Yorkers, I had gone to the Garden that night out of curiosity, standing outside in the pleasant evening air with thousands of others only to be told that the Garden was already at capacity. I didn't mind since I wasn't expecting the Korean speaker to be influential in my life.

Soon after I heard the lectures to which the Japanese woman had invited me, I was able to hear the first lecture I had missed. It explored God's motivation for creating the world and God's intended ideals for human life, especially for the family. The lectures together gave me a framework for understanding issues that had long puzzled me and provided new wisdom.

In these lectures, secular and sacred history were interwoven in a way I could respect. Science and religion came together as parts of a whole. The extent and nature of evil were no longer a mystery. The world's religions were embraced and harmonized without diminishing the worth of the Judeo-Christian tradition or any other faith. The world's religions share many of their teachings in common and could live harmoniously together.

The lectures reaffirmed my initial spiritual experience that had led me to believe that the world we live in has three basic parts: God, a spiritual world, and the physical world.

I learned that each of us has our own spiritual mind and a spiritual body that resembles us. Our spiritual selves, which live eternally, are uniquely ours and have the same five senses as our physical bodies.

We are born on earth, as we well know, and can have children here. Our physical bodies support and protect our spirits as they grow. Then we move on to the spiritual realm, a world in which people can continue to develop their relationship with God. In the spiritual world, we breathe love, which is easier for those who have lived with love on earth. Those who instead have selfishly harmed others can grow, too, repenting, compensating for the harm they have caused, and learning about God. God is a parent who hopes for everyone to be healed eventually.

As incomplete and imperfect as our scientific understanding may be, it remains an anchor in my life. The nature of our minds and our need for order, predictability, complexity, and intellectual beauty have become for me qualities we inherited from and, more importantly, share with God. As I've studied the wisdom of Rev. Moon, I have come to realize that God is reflected in the natural world more than I had previously grasped.[2]

I am delighted to have stumbled upon the understanding that is still unfolding in my life. I have come to conceive of people as members of God's one family.

I should add that as I've gotten to know others drawn to this teaching, I've discovered that many of them also had early spiritual experiences. In their dreams, they were told there was new truth to be found. A number of Christian pastors had dreams in which they saw Sun Myung Moon together with the Lord Jesus, who was his primary teacher.

---

2 Books covering Rev. Moon's thought are commonly available. The book *Divine Principle* gives a more extensive overview.

I have become aware of a living, breathing unity between God and potentially all people. I live in a higher, more purified and peaceful atmosphere than I did when I was younger.

I have enjoyed a lifetime of marriage to a husband, Lawrence David Criner, whose understanding of God I deeply appreciate.

One of the reasons I had been blocked from being fully satisfied by the theological traditions I had encountered earlier in life was that despite the rich wisdom they contain, I needed a worldview that felt more complete. Once I had that worldview, other traditions became more meaningful.

Jesus Calls Sun Myung Moon

When I first heard the lectures to which the Japanese woman invited me, I had no knowledge of the personal history that had allowed Rev. Sun Myung Moon to gain the spiritual depth and understanding that made these lectures possible.

The Lord Jesus first came to the young Moon when he was fifteen following one of many long nights he had spent on a mountainside in prayer. In his prayer, he was seeking to understand how to ease the suffering of his Korean homeland, which was enduring Japanese occupation.

Jesus asked the young Moon to follow him and eventually take responsibility for a role in healing the sin of the world. At first, Moon felt he could not fulfill such a high obligation, but as the hours passed, he realized that if Jesus was calling him, he should obey. This began a lifelong relationship between them.

The Lord Jesus came to Sun Myung Moon almost daily over a span of ten years, helping him to grasp wisdom he would need and guiding the development of his character. Through these years of their relationship, Moon based his own sinless manhood on the life of Jesus and dedicated himself to God's will alone. Their spiritual unity grew.

During this first decade, Moon prayed for answers to essential questions including the meaning of biblical passages. Often, he prayed for days in tears, as those who knew him then have reported. He searched to grasp how God could restore the world back to the original creation and to know what he should do.

Through his prayers and the Lord Jesus' guidance, he came to understand much about God's effort to heal the world. He realized that there is acute pain in God's heart as God observes the fate of people trapped in war, confusion, crime, and misery. He understood that this sorrowful situation developed as the result of human mistakes that did not need to occur. He committed himself to easing God's well of pain regardless of the personal cost. This sustained him through many hardships.

God's inner nature is a heart of true love. We were created to be God's own children who could fully embody heavenly character as the Lord Jesus does. We were to have experienced God's love and wisdom as an active presence in our spirits, in our families, and as the atmosphere of the larger world surrounding us. God wishes for us to embrace our highest potential. Rev. Moon understood that he was to help guide humanity back to God so that God's dream and our dreams could be fulfilled.

Ten years after his first meeting with Jesus, Sun Myung Moon fasted for forty days after which he was abandoned by God until he could prove himself by maintaining his convictions without spiritual support. Finally, the Lord Jesus, together with the founders of the other world religions, approved his understanding. Rev. Moon embarked on his role in God's providence as the Lord of the Second Advent.

A Great Price

When Sun Myung Moon's ministry began, World War II had ended, and he was living in the peaceful southern part of Korea. Unfortunately, the northern section of the country was now under the control of communists, and like all doctrinaire Marxists, they opposed religion and were persecuting Christians.

One day when Sun Myung Moon was on his way to the market, God called him and asked him to travel to North Korea. He was asked to go to the communist area and preach God's word to the people. This request may appear unfathomable, but there were dispensational reasons for the journey.

Ever willing to make a sacrificial offering for the future of the Christian world and the world as a whole, Sun Myung Moon also went to North Korea with hope that he might be able to replace key providential figures who had been unsuccessful. South Korean Christians God had chosen to spread Moon's teachings to the wider Christian world had been unable to do so for various reasons. The Christians most prepared to replace them were in North Korea.

Sun Myung Moon's life and thought are grounded in Christianity. A key purpose of his ministry is to fulfill God's desires as expressed in the Bible. Had the Christians that God originally prepared been able to accomplish their responsibilities and successfully communicate what they understood, Moon would not have had to undertake this perilous journey.

The North Korean city of Pyongyang, now the capital of North Korea, was known for having the greatest number of Korean Christian churches. Although the communist government installed in North Korea by the Soviet Union at the end of World War II was persecuting Christians, there was still a large number of dedicated, respected Christians living there. Among these Christians, Moon might be able to raise new followers who could communicate his mission to the wider world. If these new disciples could reach South Korea, they could testify to him. Perhaps they could create enough interest that his providence, his character, and his wisdom would be noticed and valued in the Christian world and beyond.

When I was growing up in America, the American Christians I knew were both comfortable with their faith and open to new ideas. Had they had a chance to hear Rev. Moon's teaching, especially his understanding of marriage and the family, I expect that many of them would have appreciated his thought and felt comfortable incorporating his ministry into their lives.

Moon went to North Korea clearly aware of the dangers but willing to make a sacrificial offering so that God could have a better opportunity to bless the world with new, more complete truth. Certainly, there have been moments when others on God's side have been asked to take risks, to simply stand for what they believe regardless of the consequences. Representing good despite powerful opposition has a long history in the religious world. One thinks of the early Christians who died facing lions, their act a public testimony to Jesus as Messiah.

Regardless of the underlying providential reasons for the journey, this remains a time in Sun Myung Moon's life that can be understood simply as it was lived. When Moon obeyed, he fully realized the risk he was taking. Yet because of his deep understanding of God, the Lord Jesus, and the value of Christianity with its long history of faith and sacrifice, he offered his life and went. Once there, he proclaimed God's word and was well received. The number of his followers steadily grew.

Unfortunately, he was soon reported to the police. He was arrested and tortured, but he did not renounce his faith. Enduring unrelentingly painful torture of the kind that has caused others to feel that God has abandoned them – and thus led them to abandon God – he continued to hold God in his heart.

Finally, vomiting blood and so badly wounded that his life was in danger, he seemed to his captors to be dead or dying. As a warning to others, they threw his body outside the prison. Friends who had been watching from a distance took his body expecting to prepare it for burial, but after a while, he murmured. He was slowly nursed back to health.

When he was able, he continued his mission educating followers in the communist-controlled area. Needless to say, this required immense courage. Too soon, he was arrested again, and this time, he was sent to a communist labor camp, a death camp. There the prisoners loaded bags of ammonium sulfate fertilizer. They were exposed to sulfuric acid that left festering sores in their bare hands. The sores deepened until their bones were visible. They breathed the fumes the fertilizer emitted, which damaged their lungs. Few prisoners lasted six months. They were given almost no food – none if they were unable to fulfill their work quotas.

For the first weeks of his confinement, Moon helped

other prisoners by giving away half of his own inadequate ration. The situation was so desperate that if a prisoner died while eating, the other prisoners would pry open his mouth, take out his food, and eat it.

While Moon was imprisoned in this ghastly labor camp, one in which each day brought unendurable suffering to the helpless prisoners, he had to take God's side. This meant caring not only for his fellow prisoners, often innocent faithful Christians who were suffering and dying beside him, but also remaining steadfastly committed to the salvation of the North Korean communist guards even though they were inflicting vicious cruelty on the prisoners including Moon himself.

Throughout his time in North Korea, Moon understood and cared about these enemies who were worthy of occupying the bottom of hell even as he himself suffered their ongoing brutality. In these circumstances and in others throughout his life, he had to dominate his physical body's needs with his spirit to be able to continue to unite with God.

The day before he was scheduled to be executed, Sun Myung Moon was freed from the North Korean labor camp by United Nations forces fighting the communists. The prison guards, who had been trying to kill all the prisoners before the UN forces arrived, ran away as the UN troops drew near.

Once freed, he walked back to the area of North Korea where he had been preaching and searched for his followers. By this time, nearly all of them were dead or had disappeared. He did find one young man, Won Pil Kim, who remained with him all his life. Accompanied by this young man and a fellow prisoner with a broken leg, he headed away from the communist-controlled area after much prayer for the future of God's providence in Korea and the wider world.

The man with the broken leg had an old bicycle to sit on, which they pulled and pushed, and Moon sometimes carried the man on his back. A photographer taking photos of refugees happened to photograph Moon carrying this man who was finally able to receive medical care.

Sun Myung Moon and Won Pil Kim then continued their journey and, in a southern area of Korea crowded with refugees, they built a small dwelling of rocks and cardboard. There Rev. Sun Myung Moon began again to share his wisdom.

Deepening My Religious Life

After I heard the lectures in New York City, I was invited to hear a lengthier presentation of the same contents. I did and realized that I wanted to master and teach this knowledge. I studied it and then applied to spend two years learning more about the world's religions at Unification Theological Seminary, an interfaith seminary with an interfaith faculty that Rev. Moon had founded. While I was in seminary, I had some unexpectedly good experiences.

Because the bicentennial of America's founding in 1776 coincided with my years in seminary, our seminary class created a magazine to celebrate. Called *Toward Our Third Century*, it looked at America's history from its beginnings to the bicentennial.

Between semesters, a group of us went to the Library of Congress in Washington, DC to undertake the required research. We had huge piles of books on our desks. The library staff was supportive, even going with us to search the massive conveyor belts for books we had accidentally returned that we still needed. When the next semester began, I was busy because I was one of the editors assigned to finish up the magazine. I learned a great deal from this project. My university study of American history had not adequately taken into account the role of Christianity in shaping the nation's embrace of freedom.[3]

The following summer, Rev. Moon held two large rallies to celebrate the bicentennial. The first rally was in Yankee Stadium in June. The second rally was a larger gathering in September on the lawn surrounding the Washington Monument.

The Yankee Stadium rally was titled the "Bicentennial God Bless America Festival." On the day of the rally, rain suddenly began to pour just as the stadium was filling. I have a fond memory of Rev. Ken Sudo, a teacher who had deepened my knowledge of Rev. Moon's thought,

---

[3] In an essay at the end of the book, I have discussed how the religious beliefs of America's founders contributed to the freedom and democracy that characterize America.

standing on the field quietly singing and praying in the rain. He was soon joined by Tom McDevitt, who worked with him. Tom went out onto the field and spontaneously led the thoroughly soaked crowd in cheerfully singing, "You are My Sunshine." The rain cleared in time for the festival, and about 25,000 people took part. I had a fine time.

The Washington Monument rally, "America and God's Will," was held a few months later. It included the most splendid fireworks I have ever seen. There was a display for each continent to celebrate the world from which Americans have come. We seminarians, together with many other members of our movement, had spent the summer in Washington, DC inviting people, and about 300,000 came.

At both these rallies, Rev. Moon spoke about the role of faith in God in shaping America as well as the importance of this heritage for our future. He also pointed out that since Americans come from all the nations of the world, Americans are ideally positioned to love and respect the world's people and thus contribute to world peace.

v

Rev. Sudo's Injured Shoulder

My seminary classes were held on the same campus where I had first come to learn more about Rev. Moon's thought, which is called Divine Principle. While I was in seminary, I lived across the hall from the family of Rev. Ken Sudo, whose presence at the Yankee Stadium rally I mentioned. Rev. Sudo was a superb Divine Principle teacher from Japan with whom I had studied before entering seminary. The Sudo family, Rev. Sudo, his wife, young daughter, and baby son, were among my favorite people so I spent a lot of time in their apartment talking with them and sometimes sharing a meal.

In the late fall of the first year I was in seminary, months before the Yankee Stadium rally, unfortunately

Rev. Sudo was in an accident that badly damaged his right shoulder. He was in a lot of pain, and his right hand was paralyzed. The following early spring, he went back to Japan to meet with a spiritual healer. When he returned, he was in slightly less pain and could move his fingers a tiny bit, but was unable to close his hand.

One day as I happened to be walking down the hall, he saw me and beckoned to me. "Let's pray together," he said. Like all of his other students, I had prayed with him many times.

I should mention that I had wished to help Rev. Sudo recover from his injury as soon as it had happened. For months, every morning at 4:00 am when most people were asleep, I had been praying in a cold shower. My primary prayer was for Rev. Moon's wisdom to spread throughout the world and create a world of peace, freedom, and goodness. I was praying in a cold shower because I had discovered that praying in a cold shower, a practice common to several religious traditions, helps me concentrate. At the end of my prayer, I would put my shoulder in the cold water, and pray that Rev. Sudo's shoulder could be free of pain and would recover.

When we began to pray together, I placed my hand on his wounded shoulder gently as it was still injured. What happened next really surprised me. Suddenly, I could feel in my shoulder what he was feeling in his so I was able to touch his injury without hurting him.

Healing energy came, and when we had finished praying, he could almost close the fingers of his injured hand and was in much less pain. A few days later, his wife came over and asked me about the healing. I told her about the months of prayer in cold showers.

Life with God is so interesting. In the late spring after Rev. Sudo and I prayed together for the healing of his shoulder I had another experience stemming from my wish to help him. I have considered deleting this story because it is different from our usual assumptions. Still, this is a true story so I include it.

Early one morning, as I was resting on the strong, stable floor of the seminary because of my back injury, suddenly I was seasick. Later I found out that Rev. Sudo had been out on the ocean fishing with Rev. Moon, who often prayed and meditated while on the ocean. Rev. Moon had asked him, "What happened to your seasickness?"

"I don't know," Rev. Sudo had replied, as he told me later. I knew because I had received it. This world is likely full of things God can do to help us that we might not know about until the world comes closer to God.

Meeting the Lord Jesus

My first encounter with the Lord Jesus took place while I was in seminary. Over the years, I have had three irreplaceable experiences with him. Friends I have come to know who also embrace the contents of Rev. Moon's thought have found Jesus active in their lives as well.

The Lord Jesus came to the seminary in the fall of my second year shortly after we had returned from the Washington Monument rally. Fifteen or sixteen students saw him at that time including me. The president of the seminary, David S.C. Kim, saw him, too.

My own encounter began as I was praying alone in my room. Suddenly, I was aware that the Lord Jesus was there standing a few feet behind me. I felt painfully shy and unprepared to meet him. He moved back a little. Then I felt pure spiritual love warming the back of my head, and he said, "My will to save you is stronger than your sin." Sin is whatever separates us from God. Then, Jesus was on his way to other students. The experience of his presence and the words he spoke have stayed with me and strengthened me for my whole lifetime.

My second encounter with the Lord Jesus was several years later after I had graduated from seminary. I had become friends with an African-American pastor and his wife. This couple knew a Christian healer and had invited her to come to their church. The healer dedicated her life to Christian healing, traveling the world giving healings and gathering waters from places where Christian healings have taken place.

As the healer prayed for those seeking relief, spiritually I saw the Lord Jesus himself above her. I realized that he was actually doing the healing. His selfless uninterrupted God-centered love for others makes him an open channel through which God can freely move.

Putting God and others first is almost the definition of living a life of faith. Healing, cleansing away, and overcoming our self-centered characteristics is a process. Habitual characteristics that may be lifegiving in one context may not be helpful in another. We hope to grow so that we can receive God's direction.

The third time I experienced the Lord Jesus was a few years after that. I deeply respect a friend and his wife who, like me, have embraced Rev. Moon's wisdom. This couple is sincere in their desire to serve God, but they have been limited in what they can do outside their family. They have an autistic child who is so autistic that he needs to be near at least one of his parents.

This couple wanted to worship together when a special holy wine was being offered to our movement. A pastor I know, Rev. James Stewart, who follows Rev. Moon's teaching, said he would come to their home and give a service. I went along to bring food and fancy flowers.

The service was beautiful with songs, readings, and prayers. Toward the end of the service, we took the holy wine and began to pray. Then, unexpectedly, I felt a sudden strong presence of heaven. I prayed more deeply, but the husband in the couple saw the Lord Jesus standing there with the four of us.

Afterward, I felt as if Jesus had come to comfort these parents who have sacrificed for their child. I expect that in the future, they will ably serve God in the spiritual world because of the way their hearts have grown as they have met the needs of their disabled child while still struggling to share God's providence with others.

The attention the Lord Jesus has freely given to many of Rev. Moon's followers when we are not more worthy than other Christians, encourages me to trust Jesus' support for Rev. Moon's mission.

I am still studying the Bible and the history of Christianity to deepen my understanding. Partly because the Lord Jesus has touched my life and the lives of others who follow Rev. Moon, I take for granted that Jesus called him and so, while Rev. Moon's teaching and interpretation of the Bible seem true to me on their own, I assume this is wisdom the Lord Jesus approves.

God Dwelling in the Family

Some of what Rev. Moon learned from the Lord Jesus and teaches, conforms to the most simple, ordinary understandings of life. At the center of God's original and ongoing hope is the human family, which was created to be the primary dwelling place for God's heart.

God expected to share in and enhance all the kinds of love that families enjoy. Rev. Moon's emphasis on the value of families to God – and God to families – is one of the aspects of his thought that makes his understanding seem to me broadly and naturally anchored. People generally wish to live in loving families.

God had expected Adam and Eve, the first two people with eternal souls, to grow to sinless adulthood. Then they were to be blessed by God in marriage. Their union first with God as individuals, and then with God and one another in marriage, would have been the perfection and culmination of the love God intended from the beginning.

Starting from Adam and Eve, a peaceful world filled with creativity, intelligence, love, and joy would have come into being. In the free and open communication between God and people on earth, God would have enlightened us on how to care for the natural world in which we live.

Here one is reminded of the three great blessings given to us by God that are mentioned in Genesis 1:28: to be fruitful (to know the fruits of the spirit), to multiply (to be a parent to our children as God is a parent to us), and to have dominion over the earth (a dominion of love and wisdom).

Both Adam and Eve, as the Bible tells us in Genesis, and thus all men and women, are made in God's image. The masculine and feminine aspects of God are united within God in inner harmony – the kind of harmony we wish for the couples we love and for every married couple.

Thus, it stands to reason that a couple dwelling in God's love and deeply in love with one another, can embody God's heart even more fully than either the husband or wife alone. Since the Bible already teaches that both men and women are created in the image of God, this seems more a matter of elaboration than novelty.[4]

For God's love to thrive in a family, both the husband and wife must be committed to their family. Beyond our relationship with God, who we marry is the most important decision of our lives.

The physical earth is precious to God because it is here that we are born, and it is here that we grow to maturity, marry, and have children. God does not wish for the literal destruction of the planet earth, but only for an end to sin and evil on the earth. The Bible, it turns out, is full of poetic expression and rich imagery.

---

4 As Rev. Moon has pointed out, not only marriage but much of the natural world is constructed using a "pair system" in which two different elements that complement each other are joined together harmoniously. In addition to men and women, there are male and female animals. Plants have stamen and pistol. Molecules, atoms, and particles exist through a relationship of positive and negative charges. For an atom to exist, it must have both a proton (a positive charge) and an electron (a negative charge).

Another kind of pair system that can be seen in our world consists of internal character and external form, or mind and body. People have spiritual minds and bodies that live eternally, as well as physical brains and bodies. Animals have a spiritual dimension we call "instinct" and their physical brains and bodies. Plants have inherent directive natures and physical parts, as do molecules, atoms, and particles.

Salvation Through the Marriage Blessing

God wishes for all the relationships in the human family to return to their original life-giving purposes. God cannot relate to human characteristics that are not part of the original creation, which means that God is effectively shut out of much of our lives.

In order for God's original dream to come true, a sinless couple living on earth must achieve in their lives what Adam and Eve could not. A sinless man and a sinless woman are both needed for the mistakes of Adam and Eve to be transcended. When God blessed Rev. Sun Myung Moon to his eternal bride, Hak Ja Han, in holy marriage in 1960, their wedding was the sinless union

God had hoped for Adam and Eve.

God then granted Rev. Moon's couple permission to bless other couples in a Marriage Blessing ceremony in which the original sin and personal sins of the newly Blessed couples are forgiven. This is a first step toward freeing the world permanently from the intrusion of evil that has entrapped it. After the forgiveness of original sin, original sin is not passed down to the children of the couples whose sin has been forgiven.

It is on earth that children can be born free of original sin and a sinless lineage can unfold. That is why the Lord Jesus called and raised Sun Myung Moon. The marriages of people who have already entered the spiritual world can be Blessed as well, but these couples cannot begin a sinless lineage on earth.

After the original sin and personal sins of faithful married couples is forgiven, these couples will be able to dwell together not only on earth, but in the spiritual realm as they were originally meant to, coming closer and closer to God and one another. They will eventually be united with God so that they live each moment exploring life together with God – an exciting future to look forward to.

The day when original sin could be forgiven was a day the Lord Jesus had long awaited. The honor and gratitude that Rev. and Mrs. Moon have given and will forever give to the Lord Jesus for making the forgiveness of sin possible by raising the Lord of the Second Advent and founding the Christian tradition that shaped and protected his bride is so immense it is without measure. Their appreciation of Jesus's role in establishing the Marriage Blessing is a holy treasure Rev. and Mrs. Moon will hold eternally in their hearts.

Mrs. Moon was born sinless through the spiritual accomplishment of generations of her ancestors. She grew up protected by her sacrificially faithful Christian mother and grandmother and lived without straying from the sinless life she had been gifted to receive. As God desired, she married the Lord of the Second Advent, completing the foundation God needed to begin the restoration of the world.

She went on to a lifetime of sinless marriage. She is the first woman to live without sin as God intended. She embodies the feminine nature of God and is the first woman to fully do so. How precious to God that surely is. She is also my teacher.

Rev. Moon said that creating the conditions that allowed their couple to be joined in marriage and receive God's permission to liberate humanity through the Marriage Blessing was his most difficult journey. Then one can only surmise that this journey must have been an incredibly challenging spiritual course weighed down by the accumulated sin of the world. In the end, though, thanks to Rev. Moon's single-minded dedication to God and his selfless motivation as well as the absolute purity and devotion to God of his holy bride, there was providential success, and today the Marriage Blessing is secure.

The establishment of the Marriage Blessing on earth is also the incredible celebratory moment in God's providence when the Lord Jesus in heaven is finally freed to marry his own heavenly bride. The Lord Jesus has always put God's providence for the salvation of the world first in his life. Thus, it is only fitting that he would not choose to be blessed by God in marriage unless the conditions needed for the salvation of the world were secure.

In the Bible, in the book of Revelation, there is the famous passage on the Marriage Supper of the Lamb. The joyous occasion of the Marriage Supper of the Lamb has been a part of Christian thought for two thousand years. It has had various interpretations. For some Christians, it refers to an eternal union between Jesus and his church members. For other Christians, it is the marriage of the Lord Jesus himself to his own heavenly bride, an interpretation that affirms the value of marriage to God. The Marriage Supper of the Lamb, as Rev. Moon views it, certainly includes the fulfillment of these other meanings but also assigns to that sacred moment a salvific role. It signifies the marriage of a sinless couple on earth that is the first step, a necessary step, in the restoration of the world's people back to God. These various interpretations complement each other.

I should add that Rev. Moon and his wife are a rare refreshing experience. I trust them to represent God's parental heart truthfully, so I, like other members of the movement that has grown up around them, have come to call them True Parents, or True Father and True Mother, or Father Moon and Mother Moon. I'll continue referring to them as Rev. and Mrs. Moon in this book for the sake of clarity for the reader.

Suggesting a Spouse

As is well known, Rev. Moon has suggested a spouse for many of those who follow him. It should be clarified that Rev. Moon himself does not decide these matches. He is simply a channel through which God can express a choice. Because Rev. Moon is following God and not personally deciding the matches himself, he has said that after matching a large number of couples, he is sometimes unable to remember who is matched to whom even if he is well acquainted with the newly matched individuals.

The general public has certainly wondered why thousands of young people, and older people, too, would accept Rev. Moon's suggestion for their marriages. The simple answer is that they have trusted that God, who knows their characteristics and wishes, would be deciding.

Earlier in the book, I mentioned that even before I heard Rev. Moon's Divine Principle, God granted me a mystical experience in which I felt truly understood. Now I am tremendously grateful to God to have been introduced to a husband I love and with whom I share a family I trust to be eternally ours.

Rev. Moon has mentioned that among the factors that could figure into God's choice of a spouse beyond the simple happiness of the couple might be that they could have exceptional children, or that their ancestors who were enemies could find peace through the couple's love for one another.

Sin has multiplied through such a long history of thousands of years that the present-day society that surrounds the Blessed families is filled with false values. Because of this, Rev. Moon has taught that it will likely take about ten generations of children descended from the first Blessed couple in each lineage before all the effects of the cultural bad habits and destructive circumstances can be washed away completely. If the world was filled with Blessed families, that would also help everybody to experience the joy of naturally sharing each moment with God.

Even now, I have found that my own marriage has freed me internally in ways that I especially appreciate, and I feel closer to God as a result. Many prayers have been answered. I think that couples who have fallen in love have often found that somehow the whole universe feels present when they are in their own world together. At least, this is my experience.

When original sin and personal sin are forgiven, it clears the spiritual atmosphere in which a person is living, making it easier to instinctively understand how to be good. Children without original sin may grow up in an imperfect cultural environment, but they are still capable of being naturally close to God, and their children can be even closer. Eventually, as Rev. Moon has said, people can be completely free of sin, become one with God internally, and easily manifest characteristics and talents that are inspiring.

A Difficult Mission

Soon after their Holy Marriage, God asked Rev. and Mrs. Moon as a couple to undertake an extremely difficult but necessary mission. They were asked to convince God's first enemy, the archangel Lucifer, who is mentioned in the Bible, that he could trust God's love for him, safely surrender, and begin the restoration of his character.

Rev. and Mrs. Moon's mission took decades to accomplish but, in the end, the archangel trusted them. He was finally able to understand that there had been no need for the jealousy that had led him astray. He had really had nothing to fear. He had imagined that as Adam and Eve, God's first children, became increasingly able to embody God's character, they would be nearer to God than he was, replacing him, separating him from God.

He had been the angel closest to God during the creation of the world, relaying God's directions to the other angels. As the archangel of intellect, he was then given the mission of being Adam and Eve's teacher. As he observed God's children increasingly manifesting heavenly character, instead of realizing that he was going to happily enjoy their company and receive the fulness of their love when they matured, he became fearful and jealous. Actually, he should have realized that since God cared for him, he, too, could expect a most wonderful future.

God is only goodness, and God's love is only true love. As Rev. Moon explained, of course, God's original plan for the creation included the greatest possible happiness for the angels.

If Adam and Eve could have remained sinless as individuals and had celebrated their marriage as God intended, God planned to create female angels and form couples of male and female angels as part of the joyful and glorious wedding celebration. Over time, the angels would have received fulfilling love not only from God and Adam and Eve but from a whole world of Adam and Eve's sinless descendants.

In order to successfully restore Lucifer, God asked Rev. and Mrs. Moon to give their full love and attention not only to Lucifer, but to the sinful people of the world, serving them first and foremost. This was one means by which God hoped they could convince the jealous archangel that God's love for him remained as reliable and trustworthy as it had always actually been.

In the end, Rev. and Mrs. Moon did win Lucifer's trust. They brought the archangel back to the side of heaven to begin his healing by serving others to compensate for his sins. The experience of Rev. and Mrs. Moon's pure and consistent love was finally convincing. The spiritual and physical worlds are now in a better position to heal over time.[5]

---

[5] In the biblical Garden of Eden, there are three characters and three symbols, and there is a one-to-one correspondence between them. The serpent who tempts Adam and Eve is a symbol for the archangel Lucifer, as is widely recognized. The two trees at the center of the garden are symbols for Adam and Eve. Adam is represented by the tree of life. Eve, for the purposes of this story, is the tree of the knowledge of good and evil. The fruit of this tree is all of humanity.

God gave Adam and Eve a commandment to refrain from a sexual union until they were spiritually one with God and were Blessed by God in marriage. The archangel created circumstances that succeeded in confusing and damaging them in their immaturity and resulted in their coming together prematurely. His intention was to dominate them, and he was successful in intruding himself into their previously unspoiled characters. The history of the ways that evil has multiplied in the world sadly reveals the full extent of the damage introduced into the human character. A more complete rendition of this tragedy can be found in the book *Divine Principle*.

During the course of striving to gain Lucifer's trust, Rev. and Mrs. Moon could not risk arousing more feelings of jealousy in God's first enemy. Thus, their responsibilities did not permit them to freely share their love and wisdom with their own precious children as they wished. Rev. Moon called this "a crucifixion of the heart" because he and his wife so loved, missed, and longed to be with their own children and were so painfully aware of how much their children needed them. Nevertheless, advancing God's providence for the world's restoration was their God-given mission, and thus had to take priority.

Early Days with Mrs. Moon

Both Rev. Moon and his wife have lived almost unbelievably sacrificial lives. Keeping a schedule no one else could match, they have slept only two or three hours a night. They have fourteen children. Several of the younger ones were born by caesarean section.

I recall Mrs. Moon's presence at a seminary graduation where I hoped she wasn't in too much pain from her most recent caesarean. I knew she couldn't be completely healed, but both she and her husband often transcended their pain in order to convey God's love to others. She was brave and vivacious, beautiful, and supportive of the graduates. They were her children, too.

In my early days of knowing the Moons, Rev. Moon

was more visible in the public life of the movement. He gave speeches, hosted planning meetings, taught members, and held public events.

Mrs. Moon prayed long hours for the responsibilities of their mission. Right after their holy marriage, she spent almost all her time in prayer – prayer that solidified her unity with her husband and gave her a more comprehensive understanding of their mission.

We saw her at Sunday services. While her husband spoke, she focused her attention on individual members, connecting them with her pure uplifting spirit, caring for one and then another. She joined her husband at the celebration of church holidays where they sang together, sharing the joy of the moment with everyone. At times, they were able to travel together so that the world's members could meet them both.

From the beginning of their married life, the Moons prayed sacrificially for the sake of the much-loved Christian world, hoping that Christians would be able to embrace the healing of sin that is now possible. All the years of their lives, Rev. and Mrs. Moon have hoped that Christians, and the faithful of other religions, would discover reasons to embrace God's providence of precious forgiveness and wisdom, and many have.

After all the Moons' children were born, Mrs. Moon became increasingly active on the world stage herself.

She travelled internationally to meet members, founded organizations, and embarked on speaking tours of her own around the world supported by the prayers of her husband.

She was always courageous and able to assess her situation accurately, fulfilling God's wishes even in potentially dangerous situations. Once, to my astonishment, she delivered her message centered on God in China's Great Hall of the People despite significant opposition from high-ranking members of the Chinese government.

Rev. Moon said, after a lifetime of serving God together with his wife, that if he was alone, they were both present and vice versa. Either one of them fully represents their couple.

Peace on Earth

God's intended creation was to have been a world of uninterrupted peace flowing throughout society. Thus Rev. Moon and his wife have actively pursued peace on earth.

The Lord Jesus, the Prince of Peace, had imparted his hope to Rev. Moon that Christians could put their love of God and faith in the Lord Jesus first and then harmonize their differences to form a common Christian culture.

The Lord Jesus had also expressed his wish that the Christian community as a whole would respect and reach out to all of the world's religions to bring lasting peace among them. It is God's hope that the religions come to know one another and dwell together harmoniously.

Rev. Moon taught that in order for the world's religions to have effective moral authority on the world stage, there must be an interreligious peace in which they stand before the world together. They should be a visible presence affirming the value of peace and the Golden Rule (Do unto others as you would have them do unto you), which all these faiths profess in some form. As theologians, scholars of religion, and Rev. Moon, have all pointed out, despite arising at different times and in different places, the world's religions share many, perhaps a majority, of their teachings in common.

Four of the world's major faiths have been embraced in Korea. It is a nation with a rich religious history of its own as well. Traditionally, Koreans have lived with reverence for a Higher Being. They have thought of themselves as a people of Heaven. When Buddhism, Confucianism, Taoism, and Christianity were introduced, these faiths were valued and harmonized by the Koreans so that each of the faiths could contribute its unique perspective to Korean life.

There is a deep Buddhist root in the culture that has fostered the cultivation of a peaceful, balanced mind. A Confucian tradition of loyalty and honor in the family has supported social cohesion and goodness in the larger society. Purity before marriage and fidelity in marriage are deeply ingrained. Taoism has connected Koreans to the natural world. When Christianity was introduced, it became the primary faith.

After Rev. Moon returned from being imprisoned in North Korea, he first founded the Holy Spirit Association for the Unification of World Christianity (often shortened to Unification Church) to honor the Lord Jesus' wish for greater Christian unity. Later, Rev. Moon and his wife created the interfaith Family Federation for World Peace and Unification, which offers the salvation of the Marriage Blessing to virtuous families of all faiths and to families of secular non-believers as well.

Tragically, in recent times, there has been a sharp rise in violent Muslim extremism. Muslim terrorists have murdered tens of thousands of peaceful Christians, moderate Muslims, Jews, and secular people, especially in Africa. These murders, which have been inflicted even on tiny children, continue as I write. Muslim extremists are, of course, well known in America for having destroyed the World Trade Towers in New York City and attacked the Pentagon in 2001.

Rev. Moon had earlier predicted, as I well remember, that acts of Muslim terrorism would occur in the absence of greater interreligious respect on a world level. He had hoped to prevent this tragic aggression by offering an alternative, but our movement was unable to secure the kind of interreligious harmony among the major faiths that could be clearly acknowledged by the world as a whole.

Rev. Moon wisely suggested that the United Nations add another chamber, an interfaith chamber, that would bring together the most respected religious minds from the world's faiths to set an example of unity and wisdom. This group could work to prevent and resolve religious conflicts. We tried to make this happen. While it has yet to be realized, I hope it will come to be or that other developments will accomplish the same goals.

I am grateful that there are believers in all the major religions striving for world interfaith reconciliation. One hopes that in the future the adherents of each faith will be able to appreciate all the religions and understand how to harmonize them without diminishing their unique contributions.

In his effort to bring peace among the world's religions, Rev. Moon sponsored two important interfaith volumes: *World Scripture: A Comparative Anthology of Sacred Texts*, and later *World Scripture and the Teachings of Sun Myung Moon*. These volumes lay out the extensive similarities among the faiths. They are among my favorite books. If the world's religions were to have the moral stature on the world stage that flowed from respect for one another, the religious world as a whole could provide a higher moral perspective that affirms God's virtues, a perspective that is much needed in our world.

With these goals in mind, Rev. Moon founded

international interreligious organizations that brought together religious scholars, theologians, and clergy.

Beginning in the mid-1970s when I was in seminary, Rev. Moon sponsored conferences for theologians. As interest grew, and more theologians joined, the New Ecumenical Research Association, or New ERA, was born.

Together with other members in our movement, some of whom attended the conferences, I supported these gatherings in prayer. When the proceedings of the New ERA conferences were published, and a New ERA newsletter was created, as an editor I helped to accomplish this.

Then, as interest grew, in 1981, over a hundred and fifty theologians and scholars of religion from all of the world's religious backgrounds attended the first God conference, God: The Contemporary Discussion. Sponsored by Rev. Moon, the conference was held in Hawaii where the flowers were gorgeous and the weather could not have been finer. As a staff member, I greatly enjoyed this conference. The papers were so diverse and were later published – a publishing project to which I contributed. Other exciting God conferences followed.

Rev. Moon reached out to the world's clergy. He sponsored an Assembly of the World's Religions which was attended by clergy from all the world's faiths. He developed relationships with religions figures who were seeking interreligious harmony on their own such as the Grand Mufti of Syria and the well-known scholar of world religions, Huston Smith.

Rev. Moon invited a young adult interfaith group to travel together to the holy sites of their religions. They were accompanied by Huston Smith's wife and several members of our movement, one of whom brought back gifts including a beautiful scarf from Israel that I am happy to own. As the interfaith group prayed and travelled together, they came to appreciate that they indeed shared a common heart and realized they could work with each other harmoniously.

Eventually Rev. Moon asked Jewish rabbis, Christian clergy, and Muslim imams to travel to Israel and walk through the streets of Jerusalem chanting, "Peace, Shalom, As-Salaam-Alai-Kum." For those who are not familiar with the meaning of all of these words, As-Salaam-Alai-Kum translates, "peace be unto you." Shalom conveys peace, harmony, wholeness, and tranquility. This interfaith clergy delegation was invited to the Temple Mount by the Palestinians, an atypical invitation since the Jewish rabbis were included.

Rev. Moon's outreach included his relationship with Minister Louis Farrakhan of the Nation of Islam whose extreme distrust of white people and Jews, Rev. Moon helped to lessen. In 2000, Minister Farrakhan and Rev.

Moon jointly hosted a Million Family March on the mall in Washington, DC. African-American speakers were joined by speakers from other races. Minister Farrakhan himself shared his experiences with Rev. Moon. I attended and, though I am white, I felt no hostility from the African-American crowd.

I have always been grateful for the relationship between Minister Farrakhan and Rev. Moon. It was formed before radical Islamists attacked the World Trade Towers and the Pentagon. I have wondered if more tragedies might have taken place in America if the Nation of Islam had not found a friend in Rev. Moon.

Communism and the Free World

Rev. Moon hoped to end the world's division into the free world in which God is recognized, and the communist world which denies God's existence. He wished for God to be freely acknowledged everywhere, and for people everywhere to be free and prosperous. To achieve these ends, along with other worthy goals, he thoughtfully created his own world-level reputation, one that allowed him to stand on the world stage to address these issues.

Unlike many religious figures who ignore the academic and secular worlds, Rev. Moon held conferences for professors and scientists in a variety of academic disciplines. He founded newspapers around the world.

These efforts were not only valuable in their own right, but eventually led to a cordial meeting between Rev. and Mrs. Moon and Mikhail Gorbachev when Gorbachev led the Soviet Union. Following this meeting, the Moons were able to meet with Kim Il Sung, the founder of communist North Korea.

Rev. Moon began his outreach to academics when he hosted the first International Conference on the Unity of the Sciences (ICUS) in 1968. After surmounting some initial suspicion that the conference was simply a means to draw attention to Rev. Moon's movement, a large number of scientists attended ICUS, including Nobel Prize winners.

Among the participants were Nobel laureates Sir John Eccles, Eugene Wigner, Robert S. Mulliken, and Lord Edgar Adrian. They came because they were interested in the topics for discussion: the unity of the sciences, and the relationship between science and morality, both intellectually worthy topics that Rev. Moon had selected.

Then, in 1973, Rev. Moon founded the Professors World Peace Academy (PWPA). PWPA brought together academics in the humanities from around the world who might not otherwise have had a chance to meet so they could discuss various subjects including world peace.

One famous Professors World Peace Academy conference was held in Geneva, Switzerland in 1985. Rev. Moon asked Dr. Morton Kaplan, a political science professor at the University of Chicago who was then chairman of PWPA, to hold a conference on the decline and fall of the Soviet empire and possible scenarios that would follow such a development.

At the time, Rev. Moon alone knew clearly that this collapse was coming within a few short years. At the conference, eighty Sovietologists presented papers detailing problems in the Soviet Union though most participants doubted its imminent demise.

When this conference took place, my husband and I had just moved to Washington, DC. We had recently been hired as editors for a new monthly magazine called the *World & I* owned by the parent company of *The Washington Times*, a daily newspaper in the nation's capital that Rev. Moon had founded.

As it turned out, I happened to be the editor who was responsible for publishing papers from the Geneva conference in the *World & I*. I learned quite a bit about the economic troubles plaguing the Soviet Union. Central planning that did not permit criticism had resulted in extreme inefficiencies. There was also a large and growing antiwar sentiment in the Soviet Union as the government fought to keep communists in power in Afghanistan.

Faced with dissatisfaction, in 1987, Mikhail Gorbachev reformed the election laws so that all citizens, not just

Communist Party members, could vote. The next election revealed widespread dissatisfaction with the Communist Party. Gorbachev responded by instituting reforms: *glasnost*, a policy that promoted greater transparency in government, and *perestroika*, which created more free market opportunities.

Two short years later, to everyone's astonishment, in 1989 the Berlin Wall dividing East and West Germany came down unexpectedly as the result of an incredibly fortunate error. The government of communist East Germany had decided to liberalize travel abroad and was adopting a new policy on passport applications. Gunter Schabowski, the government official tasked with announcing the new policy had not been in the meetings where it was formulated. Based on the notes he had been given, he mistakenly announced that a new policy allowing foreign travel took effect "immediately."

Crowds of people in East Germany rushed to the Berlin Wall, and although the guards were initially hesitant, they opened the gates. East Germans began tearing down the Berlin Wall itself using simple tools and even their bare hands. A warm welcome from the West Germans awaited them. East and West Germany were soon reunited. One can only fantasize and imagine the invisible hand of God in these improbable events.

The Soviet Union was dissolved a couple of years

later at the end of 1991. Bowing to the will of the peoples involved, Russia and the other nations in the Soviet Union, which included nations the Soviet Union had captured during World War II, all became independent non-communist nations once more.

Shortly before that, in 1990 Rev. Moon and his wife were invited to meet privately with Mikhail Gorbachev in his office. Rev. Moon was in Moscow attending the annual meeting of the World Media Association, an organization of journalists from all over the world including Russia that Rev. Moon had created more than a decade earlier.

By this time, Rev. Moon had newspapers in many parts of the world. He had, as already noted, *The Washington Times* in America's capital. In New York City, he had two newspapers: *The New York City Tribune* and a Spanish language paper, *Noticias del Mundo*. There was *Sekai Nippo* in Tokyo, *Segye Ilbo* in Seoul, *The Middle East Times* in Cairo, and *The Zambizi Times* in South Africa. There were smaller publications in Latin America that were incorporated a few years later into *Tiempos del Mundo*, which became available in countries throughout Latin America.

During his meeting with Gorbachev, Rev. Moon mentioned the value of belief in God and religious freedom. Though surprised at first, Gorbachev did not end their meeting as they had already formed a comfortable personal relationship. The two men spent time together even after Gorbachev was no longer in power.

After the break-up of the Soviet Union in 1991, Russia and other former Soviet bloc countries began allowing foreign missionaries to enter. Our movement sent missionaries. They taught Divine Principle and held Sunday services. Our outreach in Russia was not popular with the Russian Orthodox Church, however, which after a few years was able to legally put an end to our efforts by instituting registration requirements we could not meet. After Vladimir Putin's rise to power in 1999, the Russian Orthodox Church was officially given a privileged status through which Putin has been able to effectively manipulate it. Other religious groups in Russia are not equally welcome and face persecution.

After Rev. Moon's meeting with Gorbachev, Kim Il Sung, the communist founder of North Korea, invited Rev. and Mrs. Moon to North Korea for their historic meeting. After many years of building his own worldwide foundation, Rev. Moon had an international stature that qualified him to be Kim Il Sung's invited guest. At that time, North Korea wished to attract investment. By inviting Rev. Moon to North Korea, Kim Il Sung hoped to send a message that investing in North Korea would be safe.

Because Rev. Moon's deep faith in God led him to oppose atheistic communism, Kim Il Sung had previously tried to kill Rev. Moon so many times, even sending assassins to America when Rev. Moon lived here. When the two men finally met, though, surprisingly Kim Il Sung discovered that he actually liked Rev. Moon and felt a special kinship with him as a fellow Korean. Before Kim Il Sung died, he told his son and successor, Kim Jong Il, to "consult with Father Moon" if there were negotiations on the reunification of Korea.

The relationship between North Korea's leaders and the Moon family continues. Not long ago, Korea's current leader, Kim Jong Un, Kim Il Sung's grandson, sent flowers for Mrs. Moon's birthday and singers for one of her cultural programs. I was startled to see the lead singer bow to the floor before Mrs. Moon in a gesture of respect for her greatness as a Korean.

The reunification of Korea would help both North and South Korea. If Korea were to have the good fortune of being reunited and disarmed, it would be an auspicious location for a United Nations headquarters, a Geneva of the East. Ban Ki-Moon, former Secretary General of the United Nations, has embraced this idea of Rev. and Mrs. Moon's.

PART TWO

Sharing Life with Rev. and Mrs. Moon

Personal Experiences with Rev. Moon

There is much more to say about the significant accomplishments of Rev. and Mrs. Moon, and I will continue to include these. Now, though, I would like to share more of my personal experiences with Rev. Moon, including ways I saw him invest himself for the sake of world peace, which I haven't yet mentioned. Later, I will also talk about my experiences with Mrs. Moon.

In the time I spent with Rev. Moon, beyond striking me as selfless before God, I found him a remarkably healing presence. He gave long talks after which I felt spiritually and physically rejuvenated. He answered questions easily in a soft unthreatening manner. He was kind in ordinary and unexpected ways. He was imaginative as he shared his good humor with those of us who were around him.

It delighted me to discover that he could effortlessly read my mind. Other members have reported this experience, too. He read my mind numerous times, but here are two.

When I was a seminary student, he gathered my class for a talk on leadership. As he was speaking, my thoughts wandered to leaders who have failed to live up to the trust of the people following them. I thought about the imperfect heads of nations, of armies, of businesses. I thought about the imperfect parenting and teaching in the world.

After a while, Rev. Moon leaned toward me and, speaking to my heart, said softly, "In the kingdom of heaven, God will be free to serve the little child." It comforted me to share his hope that good leaders will be able to care for even the most powerless among us. Then Rev. Moon went on with his talk, explaining the kinds of giving he hoped we could offer others.

One unforgettable evening, some years later after I was married, Rev. Moon spoke at length about absolute spiritual fidelity to one's husband or wife. When I got home, I sat down next to my husband, Lawrence Criner, who is called Larry by his family and friends. Then amazingly, when I closed my eyes, I had a vision of beautiful little boys and girls floating in the air above us who represented the potential children of our couple. They were entrancing. I felt almost as if I had met them.

By then, I had endured miscarriages that had been emotionally wounding because I had looked forward to knowing the children I lost. The vision God gave me was a way for God to reach out and heal me. When I had gotten home, my heart was still connected to Rev. Moon's talk that evening, and I knew that was why I had such an entrancing vision.

Sometime later, I wanted to thank him when I was with him again. I was sitting around a table with other members who were talking about their public missions so I was feeling shy about mentioning my experience. Still, he knew so easily what was in my heart without my saying anything. He leaned across the table, stretching an arm in my direction, and said, "Should have been princes and princesses." I was so startled that I looked at him with a completely empty mind. When I did, I felt joy I can only describe as God's joy.

I'd also like to mention a physical healing I experienced at one of Rev. Moon's talks. One afternoon while Rev. Moon was speaking to a large gathering of seminary graduates, my legs cramped. I was sitting on the floor in the middle of a room that had become overcrowded. My legs were so painful that I could barely handle it, but I couldn't get up without being rude and disturbing other people. Then, as Rev. Moon spoke, God's presence in the room increased, becoming more and more substantial until I felt I could almost lean on it. To my relief, suddenly my pain was gone, and I was fine for the remaining hours of the talk.

Pastor in Idaho

In the fall after I graduated from seminary, I became State Leader of Idaho and the pastor for our members in Boise. This followed a few months of summer fundraising which I had very much enjoyed since my back had just healed enough that I could walk around freely all day.

The members who were with me in Idaho were good company. When we had guests, which was not often enough, I taught the contents of the lectures that had liberated me.

While I was in Idaho, once a month the State Leaders were called to a national State Leaders meeting with Rev. Moon. At one such gathering, he was standing at the front of the room not far from me speaking about a number of things. After a while, he looked over at me and said, "She's feeling better." I hadn't really been aware that I had been feeling so weighed down by my desire to share Rev. Moon's life and thought with more people more quickly than I could. One of the older members sitting in front of me turned around and looked at me. "Oh, beautiful!" he said.

I have never felt as naturally myself as I have in the times when I have been with Rev. Moon or his wife. Rev. Moon's wife, whose life work for peace I will discuss, is a person who unreservedly shares her pure, honest, loving, beautiful, forgiving motherly heart. Unity with either of their spirits is liberating. Whatever limiting habits of mind I unconsciously carry with me from my experiences in life evaporate when I am with these two people. I become free internally and connected to the vast ocean of sensitive consciousness that is God's.

At a State Leaders meeting held outdoors, as Rev. Moon was talking with us, a fly buzzed around him. He reached up and killed it, but as he did, he offered a slight bow to God to acknowledge the life of the fly. It was such a natural reaction for him that I more clearly grasped his oneness with God's creation.

At one memorable State Leaders' gathering, we were among hundreds of Rev. Moon's followers who had come to New York City to welcome in the New Year. Rev. Ken Sudo, whose shoulder I had prayed to heal, invited those of us who had arrived early to go to the beach to pray together for the coming year.

We got back just in time to join Rev. Moon and his wife who traditionally pray for the new year at the stroke of midnight. The next morning, there was a longer worship service at which Rev. Moon spoke, followed by a holiday lunch. Eventually, we began our monthly State Leaders meeting, and soon Rev. Moon invited us to play yute, a game traditionally played at celebrations in Korea.

I remember this meeting especially because Rev. Moon stayed with us for several days. At one point, we were sitting on the floor playing yute, and he was sitting there with us smiling and cheering us on. He was wearing a simple white shirt and white cotton pants. His ankles and a bit of his lower legs were visible.

At one point, he touched his lower leg with his thumb. I was startled to see his thumbprint indent too deeply and remain indented as we sat there. This wasn't a matter of ordinary swelling. The flesh in his legs had been so brutally beaten when he was tortured that his legs were still damaged. I thought about all the times I had seen him stand for long hours giving talks. How difficult that likely was, though he had smiled warmly and appeared completely strong and free. I was told later that although he did not interrupt his activities, he had headaches because of the way the bones in his head had been broken.

One of Rev. Moon's goals in life was to master his physical body, overcoming pain, the need to sleep, and hunger and thirst so that spiritually he could focus on God's will. He took the position that God's suffering was greater than his, and his desire was to comfort God.

He worked so many hours each day that those of us who spent a few days with him found ourselves exhausted. One of my good friends called him, "the man of iron" because of his lack of sleep and unwavering determination to heal God's sorrows. He and his wife lived sacrificially every day to create a world where God would be free and everyone could live together with God in peace. One of the older Korean members told me that Rev. Moon's wife was the only person who could keep up with him.

That Everyone May Eat

My husband and I were engaged by Rev. Moon in 1979. Soon afterward, the president of the seminary, David S.C. Kim, asked me to come back there to prepare theological conference proceedings for publication. These conferences were among those of the New Ecumenical Research Association (New ERA) that I mentioned earlier. They were conferences for theologians from a variety of religious backgrounds who were meeting to discuss Rev. Moon's thought and various interfaith topics. Soon the God conferences, also previously mentioned, began, and their proceedings needed to be prepared for publication. I worked on the first volume and other members took care of later volumes.

When I arrived at the seminary, my husband was there studying. He was soon to graduate. Then he went to work in Harlem where he had a close friend who was a Catholic priest. My husband drove to different companies to pick up day-old bread and other officially expired food that was still good and distribute it to Harlem's old-age homes and daycare centers.

My husband was committed to getting food to those who needed it. He had been thinking seriously about joining a United Nations team working abroad to teach people how to grow better crops. Rev. Moon offered him another way to help address hunger: ocean fishing, which my husband did for a number of years before he and I became editors.

Rev. Moon pointed out that unless everyone is fed, peace will remain elusive. He believed that feeding the world's population as it grows would be feasible if the ocean's resources were properly developed. He wanted people to learn how to fish sustainably.

Even when I was in seminary, Rev. Moon had us catching fish. First, weights were attached to the bottom of an extremely long fishing net. I remember one delicate and beautiful dawn after I had been up all night studying the Old Testament. I was drawn to the back lawn where the net was being prepared expecting that other brothers and sisters would be there. Thinking that perhaps I could help, I was surprised to find the lawn deserted except for the half-finished net. For a moment, I thought of Jesus' disciples who had been fishermen. I wondered if they were looking down on us, and what they might make of us if they were, and for a moment, I felt close to them.

The seminary grounds bordered the Hudson River and beside the river, there was a lagoon on seminary property. When the net was finished, it was taken to the shoreline. Once the tide had come in bringing carp into the lagoon, the net was dropped so the carp were blocked from going back to the river. At low tide they were easy to spot in the shallow water. Rev. Moon introduced a new way to catch them. He showed us how to catch them with our hands without hurting them.

I could only watch because my back was still injured, but the rest of my seminary class flopped around in the mud catching the beautiful carp with their hands, quickly turning the fish upside down, gently holding them between an arm and one side of their bodies with a couple fingers just inside the fishes' mouths. The fish were so utterly stunned at being upside down for the first time that they held completely still. They were carried to a waiting truck with water in the back and were transported to ponds on our properties.

Later, Rev. Moon designed fishing boats, and our members built the boats and used them. My husband, who was a captain, and his crew were among the members who spent the summers catching giant bluefin tuna in the Atlantic near Gloucester, Massachusetts. Each tuna weighed nearly a thousand pounds.

I have to include one story from my husband's tuna fishing. The boats typically went out early just as dawn was breaking. One especially gray morning as my husband was going out, he heard the sound of a large fishing boat not too far away in the distance. He stopped, not wanting to get too close and not completely sure where it was. He asked one of his crew to lie in the front of their boat to see if he could see anything. Just as this crew member lay down, a whale came up right in front of the boat with its mouth open. Needless to say, the crew member was startled. He said he had been imagining the Loch Ness monster when the whale came up. I should add that whales can have really bad breath.

Later, Rev. Moon established a fishing fleet that still fishes the waters off Alaska. These boats catch and sell wild fresh healthy Alaskan fish that comes from clean water. Rev. Moon also created a long-lasting fish powder to give to people facing starvation.

I Go Fishing with Rev. Moon

My husband and I were engaged for three years and then we were one of the couples married in a large wedding Rev. Moon held in Madison Square Garden in 1982. During the time we were engaged, we corresponded but were seldom together as our missions were in different places. I was working on publications at the seminary, and my husband was spending most of the year as an Ocean Church leader first in Savannah, Georgia and then in Boston, Massachusetts, except for the summers when he was tuna fishing in Gloucester.

In the summer after our wedding, my husband went bluefin tuna fishing as part of a small group Rev. Moon took with him to Provincetown, Massachusetts. The other members continued fishing in Gloucester.

One evening, my husband was out walking on the beach not far from the home in Provincetown where Rev. and Mrs. Moon were staying. There he met Mrs. Moon who was also walking on the beach. Ever generous, she picked up a round white rock and, with a loving smile, gave it to my husband as a gift. My husband thinks of nature as God's cathedral. Thus, her gift was especially welcomed.

I happened to be in New York City when I got a call from my husband. Rev. Moon had invited a few of the fishermen's wives to join them. I took a bus and arrived in Provincetown in the early hours of the morning. My husband picked me up, and we drove down to the dock. Rev. Moon had not yet returned from tuna fishing all day and striped bass fishing all night. Finally, around 9:30 am, his boat came in.

The fishing crews scattered, including my husband. They went off to fetch and load bait and do other chores. I walked down to Rev. Moon's boat. Another wife was already there along with the boat captain, two older Korean members, and one of my Japanese friends from seminary. About half an hour later, Rev. Moon came down the dock and was ready to go back to sea. We just went out immediately with everyone who was on the boat.

As we were getting ready to go, Rev. Moon paused to

ask me if I love my husband. I do love my husband, but at the time we were still getting to know each other. Slowly, I nodded, "Yes." He said that wasn't what he meant, but it was time to go fishing. After we had arrived at our fishing spot, one of the older Korean members suggested I go up and talk with Rev. Moon who was on the boat's upper deck.

I went to the ladder leading to the upper deck and asked if I could come up. "Yes," he said. There were two seats on the upper deck and a small table. When I had seated myself, Rev. Moon began explaining that fishing can support a family. He told me how much the striped bass he had caught the night before were worth.

Then he talked about the ocean which, like the land, has animal life, plants, and minerals. He expressed how important caring for the oceans and providing healthy fish will be for the future well-being of humanity.

As we sat talking, I felt as if the ocean around us was singing. I had been fishing once before on this boat when Rev. Moon wasn't there. The other guests who were with me on that trip had gotten seasick so I had been the only one chumming (throwing dead fish into the water to attract tuna) when a giant bluefin tuna came and bit the hook. I could feel it coming to me, but, of course, I can't land a thousand-pound tuna. The captain used the boat to fight the tuna and brought it aboard. It was a fine day.

I even got to see the whales jumping out of the water singly and in pairs. Still, I have to add that the ocean was not singing the way it was when Rev. Moon was on the boat.

As Rev. Moon and I talked on the boat's upper deck, I was feeling increasingly comfortable and nearer to God as I usually did when Rev. Moon was there. I began to think more naturally and even breathe more easily. As I relaxed, we came to a point in the conversation when I felt I could say something personal. I expected that this would be the only time I would ever be able to talk with Rev. Moon by myself so I had better say the most important thing I could possibly say. "You know, I really like your second son," I said. I could imagine Rev. Moon and this son, Heung Jin Moon, a teenager, together in a high spiritual realm.

"Pray," Rev. Moon replied, "Maybe you can have one like that."

Now if Rev. Moon could say this to me, truly he could say this to anyone who follows his teaching. I realized in that moment that he hoped we would pray to have the best children we could have. I also realized that he was more invested in heavenly lives for the children of his followers than I had realized.

Later that night, actually in the middle of the night, I had yet another unforgettable experience. Rev. Moon went out in a small boat to catch striped bass and to pray and meditate. Each of us on the larger boat took turns listening to the radio in case he needed help. When it was my turn, I alone was awake and responsible for his safety. The night was calm and the moonlight was beautiful, and as I sat there, I could hear the water lap against the side of the boat. During those hours, I felt connected with Rev. Moon as if he was the only person on earth.

Rev. Moon's Second Son

Heung Jin Moon, Rev. Moon's second son, was the first of his children to touch my heart. I had seen him from time to time when, as an older child and then a young teenager, he had visited the seminary. "Oh," I had thought, with the giddy abandon of a three-year-old, "Heavenly Father, what a fantastic human being! You must feel so hopeful!"

This young person could relate easily to all the different kinds of people around him. He was unassuming. He had a way of naturally accepting everyone and lifting them up with his goodness. I can remember thinking that if everyone in the world could meet him, through him they would surely wish to welcome God into their lives.

A year and a half after I had spoken with Rev. Moon, this precious son, who was only seventeen at the time, was killed in a tragic automobile accident. He had swerved to the right to take the full force of an oncoming truck that was out of control and had crossed into his lane. By swerving, he had saved the lives of the friends who were riding with him.

After the accident, his parents honored his life as a victory of love. As those who knew him, and spoke about him, were aware, he had always in a natural way loved the world and been willing to give his life to serve its future. He cared about the success of God's providence and wanted to help and protect his parents. Together with many other church members, I can remember thanking God that someone this good could have lived.

Yet for months I found myself continuing to grieve. I had taken for granted that some of God's hopes for people on earth would come true through this young man's life. I was deeply saddened that such a wonderful person had died, and when I thought about it, I got tears in my eyes. When I was first introduced to the husband of a woman I knew, he surprised me by telling me he had dreamed of me crying.

I am aware that everyone lives eternally and that Heung Jin can and does do good works in the spiritual world. Over the years, I've heard reports about some of them, especially his concern for our ancestors. I expect that in his open-hearted and kind way, he responds to the prayers of people who turn to him and takes care as much as possible of those who may need the guidance and comfort he can provide.

A Good Life

I have talked about Rev. and Mrs. Moon's urgent desire to feed the world. I should also mention that I learned how to care for my own health because of another of their interests. One year, I wrote advertising for the Korean Il Hwa Ginseng Tea Company, which is owned by our group. Because I was writing advertising, I read the available research on ginseng. Ginseng root is shaped like a human being, which is quite apt since it is especially healthy for people.

Ginseng is an adaptogen and thus has many functions. It can assist the body in carrying oxygen to the cells and removing impurities. It can help us relax but also quickly pump adrenalin into our bodies when it's needed. It has other properties. Learning about ginseng was the beginning of my journey toward realizing the value of eating organic food, drinking pure water, and using natural remedies.

I also thoroughly enjoyed another quite different kind of happiness. During one period in our movement, some of the older Korean members were reporting that if we gave donations, God might find a way to return the money to us. Of course, no one should think of this chance as a good reason for giving money, but actually there were two surprising occasions when my donations were repaid.

Once I offered money to an elder Korean member who wanted to take a trip abroad to invite some highly placed people to come to America for a special event. To my utter astonishment, soon afterward I received four credit card offers. Each credit card had a $300 cash bonus. The total was exactly the amount of my offering, and I enjoyed spending the money on a trip for my son and his wife.

The second time, I had attended a speech by one of Rev. Moon's daughters-in-law. Afterward I was standing around thinking that I wanted to make a donation for witnessing. Across the room, an elder Korean member who is spiritually gifted read my mind. Spiritually, he asked me how much I wanted to donate. Spiritually, I told him. Later, I made the donation and soon I received a prize for that amount.[6]

---

6 I have had several experiences in which I clearly understood

Beyond the luxury of learning about health and the joy of living in a community that was a source of pleasant surprises, both my husband and I were fortunate to enjoy top flight professional growth.

My husband, who is a marvelous match for me and someone with whom I have shared love in a lifelong marriage, was not only a good fishing boat captain. He developed into an excellent nature photographer. He wrote for Rev. Moon's newspaper in New York. Then, as I have mentioned, he and I both became magazine editors. We worked for many years at the *World & I* magazine. My husband received two Silver Gavel Awards from the American Bar Association for his coverage of legal issues in the *World & I*. During these years, my husband wrote commentaries that were published in *The Washington Times*, *The Washington Post*, and *The Wall Street Journal*.

---

words communicated consciousness to consciousness. The high realms of the spiritual world are so clear that it is not difficult to know what another person is saying spiritually.

A Good Community

Over the years, our family developed lifelong friendships among the members in our movement here in America and abroad. One of the crew members on my husband's tuna fishing boat is now in Malawi, and we are still friends and correspond. I feel close to members in Ukraine, Pakistan, Japan, and Korea. Wonderful members we know have helped our movement in Togo, Senegal, and other countries.

Here in America, we have shared our homes, our food, our money, and our clothes. We have contributed our talents to help each other. We have celebrated the successes of each other's children.

In America, there is so much diversity in our group that it is surprising that we could have met and gotten to know each other. Our members here come from all over the world and from every religious background. Those who follow Rev. and Mrs. Moon have become citizens of the world in a sense, and our children mingle freely.

My husband and I are fortunate to be part of this substantial community, one in which people lift others with their prayers. I hope that our one "family of God" can contribute to international understanding and acceptance. Living as I do it is easy to imagine how fine the world would be if the world's people were friends.

I should add that over the course of my life I have met inspiring individuals outside of our movement who decided to welcome others without prejudice. This was true of African-Americans I met in the civil rights movement. It was also true of African-American Christians I met years later. I don't want to leave this subject without mentioning the giving heart of two among those who graciously welcomed me into their lives.

Everyone is aware of how much racial discrimination African-Americans have endured and sometimes still endure, so one thing that continues to amaze me is how kind and unprejudiced a number of African-Americans have chosen to be.

One experience that stayed with me through the years was the generosity of an African-American Christian woman I met as I was handing out flyers inviting people to an interfaith program. It was an extraordinarily hot summer day. "Hello," I said, as I saw her in her front yard. We talked about the program.

She had just finished cooking, and she invited me in to eat and cool off. I will never forget her. She was so unassuming, soft-hearted, and gentle. With no hint of prejudice, she welcomed me and fed me. Together we shared God's presence.

Another African-American stranger, a young Christian woman who turned out to be a fellow school teacher, stopped in a large parking lot to offer me a ride to my car just as it was starting to rain. I hesitated to get into her dry car because I was already beginning to get wet, but she welcomed me in. She wanted to help me because she saw that I was elderly and moving slowly, and it was raining.

The American pastors who understand the work of Rev. and Mrs. Moon include remarkable African-American pastors together with the pastors from other backgrounds. All these pastors are part of a worldwide gathering of clergy and prophets from many faiths, races, and nations who appreciate the teachings on the family, the value of the Marriage Blessing in solving sin, and the interfaith work for peace of Rev. and Mrs. Moon. These clergy have joined together to form an international fellowship, the World Clergy Leadership Conference.

Persecution

Rev. Moon and his wife have been appreciated and continue to be supported by quite a large number of famous and worthwhile people around the world. The Moons have also been misunderstood and senselessly persecuted, which is exceedingly painful for me.

In America, Rev. Moon was charged with and actually convicted of tax evasion when nothing could have been farther from the truth. He had not personally prepared his taxes, and when it turned out that he owed additional money – about $7000 – he naturally offered to pay what he owed. Normally in these kinds of tax cases, all that is needed to resolve them is the correct payment. He was in Korea from which there was no extradition when the issue came to light, but he returned to the United States expecting to clear his name.

After he was convicted and sentenced to prison for tax evasion in a case that reeked of persecution, Rev. Joseph Lowry of the Southern Christian Leadership Conference and Rev. Jerry Fallwell of the Moral Majority both defended him along with more than a thousand other pastors. Senator Orin Hatch held hearings and concluded that it was unreasonable to have expected a foreigner to understand the details of American tax law.

The taxes Rev. Moon owed were a tiny sum compared with the fortune that our worldwide movement has invested in America. Critics have even persecuted Rev. Moon for being a rich man when in truth his personal lifestyle was unusually simple. Some have argued that the purpose of the tax case was to encourage Rev. Moon to stay in Korea and abandon his activities in America, but being innocent, he returned here.

When Rev. Moon was freed from prison, my husband and I, who by this time were editors in Washington DC, joined fifteen hundred other people, the vast majority of whom were pastors, some accompanied by their wives, to share a celebratory meal at a DC hotel in his honor.

Rev. Moon and his wife have been misquoted and misrepresented at other times, too, with an ignorance I have found astonishing. Rev. Moon's words have even been twisted into their opposite meaning. Rev. Moon has been portrayed as wishing for personal power when his desire is totally the opposite. He has offered his life for the sake of others.

As a religious leader, Rev. Moon is fundamentally oriented toward the restoration of God's original creation, a world in which people will not need leaders because they will be able to communicate with God directly.

Rev. Moon has wished for God to be understood through his teaching and has expressed confidence that someday his words honoring God will be widely appreciated as truthful. He has not sought personal power any more than the Lord Jesus ever sought it. Rev. Moon has only hoped for people to understand God's wisdom, and for everyone to have the internal freedom that virtue brings. Although he speaks at times in English, he is not a native English speaker, which has sometimes made it easier for those with a confused understanding or hostile intentions to twist his words.

Rev. Moon believes in freedom of the press so he chose not to directly influence the contents of the newspapers he founded. There were certainly times when I wished he had since he had much better values and judgment than some of the writers.

I was amazed to find a critic writing in *Rolling Stone* claim that Rev. Moon did not believe in global warming because a writer published in *The Washington Times* doubted it. For years, both Rev. Moon and his wife have been active champions trying to halt global warming by encouraging the development of environmentally friendly sources of energy. Our movement publishes *The Earth & I, Loving Nature, Healing the Earth*, a bi-monthly magazine that reports developments impacting global environmental issues.

I have read the online critics of Rev. Moon and the testimonies of former members who have had bad experiences in our movement. When the movement was new, some of those who joined and even some who led small activities lacked the foundation they needed to understand the basic religious values of the movement. They made all sorts of claims that were expressions of foolishly miraculous thinking and uttered grandiose proclamations with no foundation, or were too narrow, self-centered, or bossy, and they hurt others. There were members who unduly pressured others to do more fundraising and witnessing when not everyone is suited to these missions. A few who joined went back to using drugs and betrayed their marriages by being violent, behavior that is not tolerated in our movement and should never be tolerated.

I don't believe that Rev. or Mrs. Moon were aware of these individual's problems. The worldwide movement is too large. The Moons could only express general guidelines for the members to follow.

On the subject of violence, I want to add that Rev.

Moon mentioned more than once that we should refrain from hitting our children. Though it is not an absolute prohibition, it is close to one. Non-violence and good communication are general family values to be taken seriously by the parents among his followers.

Over the years, there has always been a majority of members with good character and good judgment. Quite a few are unusually virtuous, and that percentage has only increased. More members have seminary educations and/or years of living life immersed in God's wisdom. I hope that someday God will find a way to heal the good people who wanted to join but found themselves too mistreated, misinformed, and misunderstood to be able to stay.

There are still rumors about what Rev. and Mrs. Moon have supposedly said, false accusations against them, and fictions created about them and their motivation. There has been some recent persecution in Korea and Japan. This persecution rests on misinformation and misunderstanding, and in some instances, outright hostility to religious freedom, and I hope it will soon be resolved.

The misunderstanding and even dishonesty that have dogged Rev. Moon and his wife have blocked the path of many good people in the world who would find themselves spiritually comfortable with Rev. and Mrs. Moon as people and with their teaching. The Lord Jesus, as we know, also endured misunderstanding and persecution when he was alive on earth. Eventually, though, God's truth emerges.

After many years of association, I am comfortable that I know who Rev. and Mrs. Moon are. I hope everyone in the world will eventually enjoy a deep personal relationship with their wisdom and spiritual strength, their holiness, and their kindness.

Rev. Moon Ascends to the Spiritual World and Comforts Me

I so vividly remember Rev. Moon saying during one of his later public gatherings that he wanted to give his life for the sake of world peace. Others around me seemed to be calmly assuming that he was talking about his life's work for peace with which we were all familiar.

Yet in that moment, I somehow sensed that he was talking about his own untimely death. That evening, I looked up suddenly as I heard him say it. When I looked up at him, I felt that despite being in a room full of people who greatly respected and loved him, he was profoundly far away and alone.

Given the potential for conflict in the world and with many faithful religious believers, especially in Africa, facing persecution, violence, and even death, I felt that despite being elderly, he was committed to giving the struggle for peace his sacrificial dedication. I felt he wanted to contribute whatever he could and was so serious that he would give and give until he ultimately gave his life.

I thought about his sacrificial commitment to peace when in 2012, suddenly he collapsed. Physically he was so exhausted that following a fairly short illness, he died unexpectedly.

After my experience at the gathering where I had first felt that Rev. Moon would literally end up offering his life for world peace, I had started eating one meal a day. I was fasting for twenty-two hours a day because I wanted to support and honor him.

On the day he died, I was momentarily puzzled. Is this a Holy Day? I wondered. It is the tradition of our movement that we don't fast on Holy Days: True God's Day, True Parents' Day, True Children's Day, True Day of All Things, and other Holy Days.

Privately then I simply decided that the day Rev. Moon died was such a momentous occasion that it must be a

Holy Day. I took a bite of blueberries. As I ate them, to my delighted surprise, he was there beside me spiritually, eating blueberries in the spiritual world together with me, smiling, almost teasing me in an encouraging way.

I have mentioned that Rev. Moon spreads good humor and has a gentle side, and he can be remarkably healing in a fatherly way. Later, when a much-loved tree in my front yard died, and the tree company came and began to cut it down I went inside my house, and thought about the tree for a moment. Goodbye, old friend, I thought quietly.

In that moment, Rev. Moon was there with me again, spiritually sharing my heart as parents do, which allows their children to heal. Because of the lives and providence of Rev. and Mrs. Moon, I'm convinced that someday God will be able to be everyone's parent in that personal way.

Another day after Rev. Moon was in the spiritual world, I prayed an especially long prayer for God to be with the people around the world who are suffering, dying in war, starving, trapped, sick with fear, and losing their family members. After I had dried my eyes, slowly it dawned on me that it was lunchtime. When I eat, I tend to be grateful for the bright and beautiful natural world, but at that moment, simply celebrating God's creation didn't feel righteous when so many people are so desperately miserable. Then spiritually Rev. Moon was there with me again. As I put food in my mouth, he showed me that even as he eats, he holds the taste of hunger in his mouth, never forgetting them.

I feel that Rev. Moon has fully given, and in the spiritual world will continue to give his life for the sake of peace in the human soul and peace in the world. Spiritually through Rev. and Mrs. Moon, I have had moments of being surrounded by God's own pure inner peace. This experience is so substantial and is such a welcoming universe in which to dwell that it genuinely satisfies, as many Christians know. Once experienced, one wishes to stay there forever with God, our wonderful Heavenly Parent, our own Heavenly Father and Heavenly Mother harmonized together in one Heavenly presence. We want to stay in the secure "peace that passes understanding" as the Christian churches express it.

Mother of Peace

Near the end of his life, Rev. Moon said that Mrs. Moon still needed to master "five percent" to be able to lead the movement after he had gone to the spiritual world. Sensing he would die soon, he urgently wished for her to grasp the things she must know. Before he died, he said she was ready to lead, and he left everything in her hands.

Rev. Moon's wife, the gracious, lovely Dr. Hak Ja Han Moon, now continues their mission. Throughout the world, her reputation as the "Mother of Peace" is growing steadily. Having gotten to know her through the years, I trust her relationship with God and her approach to healing the world's problems, and I am extremely grateful for her.

She is the first sinless person to represent the pure

motherly aspect of God that God had originally hoped would be embodied in Eve and in all the women of the world. Since Mrs. Moon's spirit is so genuinely kind and caring, many people in the movement are like me in wishing to be close to her spiritually. She is loving. She quickly lifts people. God clearly guides her in her life and mission.

Yet even I who have always respected and loved her have found that I still am not fully aware of the nature and extent of her role in saving the world. Once in prayer I confided to Rev. Moon that I wished everyone could know how great Mrs. Moon, God's pure daughter, really is. Rev. Moon, to my surprise, replied encouragingly from the spiritual world, "I will be able to tell them." Then, I realized that I hadn't yet grasped the full extent and value to Heaven of the salvific mission to which God has called her.

Today she is the person on earth most responsible for advancing God's providence of salvation through the Marriage Blessing. In that capacity, she has been welcomed by many of the religious and political leaders of the world. Couples residing in the nations guided by these leaders have then been able to receive God's Blessing on their marriages.

She is also a miracle worker. Here is one example: Having myself once made an especially sacrificial offering in support of a providential purpose, I was surprised to find her gently asking me spiritually what I would like to receive. I said, "I would like to meet a person who wants to join our movement." Though Mrs. Moon was thousands of miles away, she found a good person for me to meet and told me where to go.

Mrs. Moon is moving the providence of God's forgiveness forward throughout the world. As she fulfills God's will, she is so selfless spiritually that she naturally helps others. She is honest and kind in that way that good mothers are. She is genuinely concerned about the well-being of the people of the world. Mrs. Moon's life and accomplishments are already remarkable.

I am confident that Rev. and Mrs. Moon can talk with each other whenever they wish, though he is now in the spiritual world while she remains on earth. I am especially convinced because Rev. Moon has spoken to so many of the movement's members since his transition, including me. When Mrs. Moon prays publicly today, I can feel her love for her husband and his presence in her heart.

Recently I came across one of her testimonies about her relationship with her husband in the spiritual world. She said, "Although my husband … has passed away to the heavenly realm, not a day goes by when I do not feel his warm presence and his guidance." She is supported by his encouragement: "You were not only my beloved wife … but my most faithful and closest disciple. … I am with you now, just as much as before."[7]

Certainly Mrs. Moon understands God's directions and the nature of the world around her. She gives public talks and expresses God's hope for peace in well-attended conferences and meetings. Her ability to express God's hope for a world free of sin has been well received

Mrs. Moon has, as I previously mentioned, travelled the world for years speaking for peace and encouraging people to live as one family loved by God. When Rev. Moon was still on earth, he spiritually supported his wife on her tours, praying she would have a significant substantial presence in the world, and indeed her work for world peace has drawn influential support.

The Honorable Ban Ki-Moon, former Secretary General of the United Nations, whose relationship to the Moons I mentioned earlier, was the first head of her international think tank, Think Tank 2022. It was named for its two thousand twenty-two founding members. These participants come from most of the world's nations: heads of state, parliamentarians, professors, and clergy from all the world's religions. The think tank is the fruit

---

[7] Excerpt from a speech by Mrs. Moon delivered by her son Kwon Jin Moon on August 21, 2013, during the opening plenary session of an International Leadership Conference at the Sheraton Walkerhill Hotel, Seoul, Korea.

of her husband's many years of work for peace as well as her own.

Africa is especially close to Mrs. Moon's heart. She hopes that Africa will be blessed to prosper spiritually so that it will be recognized worldwide as the "mother continent." Her heart cherishes the dedication to spiritual life that flourishes there despite famine, poverty, wars, and other ills.

Former African heads of state including Goodluck Jonathan of Nigeria, a Christian, and Macky Sall of Senegal, a Muslim, support and work with her. The nation of Sao Tome and Principe was the first nation in which all the families, including the president's family, participated in the Marriage Blessing. I saw photos from a large Marriage Blessing in Zimbabwe, a time of happiness that prompted me to shed tears of gratitude after all the painful turmoil that people in Zimbabwe have experienced. Later, an even larger Blessing was held in South Africa. Many other African nations have embraced the Marriage Blessing for their citizens.

I am deeply moved by Mrs. Moon's prayers for heavenly spiritual healing for the Africans who for centuries passed through the Door of No Return in Senegal on their way to a life of slavery. There is a plaque for Mrs. Moon on the wall at the Door of No Return, together with those for Nelson Mandella and Pope John Paul II.

Mrs. Moon's prayers for the healing of the souls of the millions of Cambodians slain by the communists who came to power in Cambodia after America pulled out of Vietnam are also among her unforgettable prayers. Cambodia has hosted a Marriage Blessing ceremony as have many other non-African nations.

Mrs. Moon's first organization, Women's Federation for World Peace (WFWP), has chapters all around the world. One of the activities of the Women's Federation for World Peace that has especially moved my heart is the Bridge of Peace Ceremony.

In these ceremonies, women from nations that are or have been enemies cross a Bridge of Peace coming from opposite sides. In the middle of the bridge, each woman meets a sister from the other side. These pairs of women then get to know each other and work together to promote peace and healing in their nations.

Well-known women have walked across the Bridge of Peace. Most famous is Barbara Bush, wife of former U.S. President George H.W. Bush. Mrs. Bush welcomed a Japanese sister to mark the 50th anniversary of the end of World War II. I have been moved sitting in the audience at these events.

Today Women's Federation for World Peace (WFWP) is an NGO at the United Nations. There WFWP works with the Universal Peace Federation (UPF), another NGO founded by Rev. and Mrs. Moon.[8]

The current president of our seminary, Dr. Thomas Walsh, once led the Universal Peace Federation. In this role, I recall him meeting with Pope Francis at the Vatican, accompanied by Tageldin (Taj) Hamad, today's UPF leader.

Our seminary, formerly Unification Theological Seminary, has under Dr. Walsh's leadership been renamed HJ International Graduate School for Peace and Public Leadership. The HJ stands for the Korean word "hyojeong" or "filial heart" — in this case, the heart that honors God.

Mrs. Moon is a mother to the world, living to heal the world.

---

8 Both the Women's Federation for World Peace (WFWP) and the Universal Peace Federation (UPF) are organizations that hold General Consultative Status with the UN's Economic and Social Council (ECOSOC). This allows them to participate in the discussions on peace and sustainable development. WFWP focuses on the situation of the world's women and on promoting healthy family values to contribute to a peaceful global society. UPF develops programs that support interfaith peacebuilding, sustainable development, conflict resolution, and strong families.

Cheongpyeong Holy Ground

✿✿✿✿✿✿✿

Our movement's main Holy Ground is in Korea. It is called Cheongpyeong Holy Ground because it borders Cheongpyeong Lake. Today, exceptionally beautiful buildings grace Cheongpyeong Holy Ground – more buildings than I can name.

There is an exquisite cathedral, the Cheon Won Gung, with its holy sanctuary, the Cheon Il Sanctum. This sanctified house of worship is a place where the world's people will be able to meet with God through the centuries.

Mrs. Moon dedicated the Cheon Won Gung on April 13, 2025 with a formal service broadcast around the world. Earlier, she had made sacrificial offerings inviting God to dwell in that heavenly place so that God's blessings will be able to reach out even more abundantly to the world's people.

Today in Cheongpyeong, in addition to the cathedral, there is a prayer hall and a large lecture hall. Rev. and Mrs. Moon's family have a home. A hospital, beautiful gardens, an aviary, restaurants, shops, and a Korean tea house grace the property. We have a stadium at Cheongpyeong that seats twenty-five thousand people. We even have a spacious, environmentally friendly boat on Cheongpyeong Lake that ferries passengers on tours.

Years ago, when I first went to Cheongpyeong, it was exciting to be there, but it was simple in its physical accommodations. We slept on the heated floor – Koreans commonly heat their floors – in the same room where in the morning we would roll up our sleeping bags and gather to pray and hear lectures.

As I write, these days there is a weekly worship service broadcast internationally from Korea. Tens of thousands of members around the world tune in. During the service, I have seen videos of the stadium at Cheongpyeong filled with our members, and I am truly grateful for each one of them. Also shown are videos of the members' current activities in many parts of the world.

The international worship service is broadcast from the Cheongpyeong lecture hall. Praying there during one of my trips to Cheongpyeong, I had a deep experience of

God's presence that I will never forget.

Participating in these internationally broadcast services are tens of thousands of young adults throughout the world. These are our grown Blessed children and new young members. Dedicated to God's providence, they sing and pray with amazing fervor. They evangelize in their home countries or are missionaries in foreign countries.

Mrs. Moon calls these young followers "pure water, pure flowing water." Like pure water, their presence in the world helps to cleanse it. They understand and can represent the value of purity before marriage and fidelity in marriage. They honor their Blessed Marriages, or Blessed Marriages to be. They know that together as husbands and wives centered on God's love, each couple will enjoy an ever-closer parent-child relationship with God, so they wish to spread the Marriage Blessing to others.

They are aware that the children and grandchildren of all Blessed couples can be born ever closer to God through the generations. Each family can become a more complete image of God through the healing of sin and through love and understanding. That is when life is at its best.

Mrs. Moon has also bequeathed prayer rooms, the Cheon Shim Won, or "Garden of the Original Heart," to our churches around the world. Each church in America now has its own Cheon Shim Won.

America's central church is in Las Vegas, a city that Rev. Moon chose hoping it could have a better future. There the Cheon Shim Won has an especially clear spiritual atmosphere. It was once a place where Rev. and Mrs. Moon themselves lived and prayed. When I was praying there not so long ago, Rev. and Mrs. Moon's second son, Heung Jin, spoke to me spiritually for a moment in such a kind brotherly way so as to lift my spirits and let me know he has not forgotten me. I could feel that Hyo Jin, his older brother, who is also in the spiritual world, was there together with him.

PART THREE

REFLECTIONS ON GOD'S PROVIDENCE

Spiritual Growth

Before I finish, I'd like to share some reflections on my life with Rev. and Mrs. Moon.

From the start, the time I was able to spend with them was a time of high, free spiritual life. Most of the members in our movement have had similar experiences. In person, Rev. and Mrs. Moon are a heavenly presence. As I connected with them, I found my prayers lifted to a high heaven spiritually.

In the early years after I heard Divine Principle, I was so content that without being especially conscious of it, I felt whole. I was wrapped in the moral and intellectual freedom the theology had brought me. I was focused on studying the world's religions at the seminary and accomplishing my responsibilities — bringing guests to programs, publishing papers, and other movement activities.

Then, as time passed, increasingly I hoped to live more closely connected with Rev. and Mrs. Moon themselves and to be spiritually guided by God through them. Like so many other members of their movement, little by little I developed a relationship with each of them, as I have mentioned. Their earliest followers include men and women who have remarkable spiritual clarity through unity with them.

While Rev. Moon is much closer to heaven than I am, he is never far spiritually from the people who value him. These days at any given moment when I'm focused on connecting with him, I find him predictably there, the same strong, dependable heavenly spiritual presence. I am anchored by his reliably unchanging character centered on God. I trust his unconditional love for humanity to be steady and present. He has unshakable internal courage.

Over the years, I have come to relate to him as an irreplaceable spiritual father for the world's people. I feel confident that he will personally be present with those who come to know him in the future. He will be there just as the Lord Jesus is.

I remain more grateful than I can express for the love and unwavering support Mrs. Moon has so upliftingly given her husband, and the love she is now sharing with the world. She fills a role nobody else could have come close to fulfilling. God's holy wish for a sinless married couple on earth that could secure the salvation of humanity became a reality because of her pure heavenly life as well as her husband's absolute personal commitment to God and his inheritance from the Lord Jesus.

Like her husband, Mrs. Moon stands as a major figure on God's side because she is the first sinless woman. She has touched my heart, and I think of her as a trusted spiritual mother. I hope she will be known as the wonderful person she is by all the world's people.

Rev. and Mrs. Moon share God's love and the wonders of God's pristine original creation with the people around them. They spread joy so as to relieve God's grief over the sorrows of the world. They embody the nature of God's original creation in which they dwell. Every time I experience the pure original world through their lives, I am struck by the clarity I feel, which renews my hope that someday everyone will be able to live as God originally intended.

God's unchanging desire is for true selfless love to prevail everywhere so that only the original creation remains. It is easy to understand why this continues to be God's hope. As the parent of each person, God wishes to restore everyone ever born so that only heaven exists on earth and in the eternal spiritual world. God intends for every human being to eventually be able to experience the companionship and wonder of living surrounded by God's presence. We were created to live daily enjoying God's moment-to-moment communication with us, experiencing God's marvelous love and creative imagination.

While people must repent and may have to pay a price for the harm they have done to others, people are not condemned to an eternally-lasting damnation – though it may feel that way to some egregious sinners. God's judgment is called "eternal" because it flows from God's eternal, unchanging, original nature.

Rev. Moon so completely forgave his enemies that he once saved the life of a man who had tortured him.

Internal Selflessness and Absolute Purity

When I first met Rev. Moon, I sensed his warmth and kind, stable love and concern for others, but I had never imagined anyone so totally selfless. Centered internally on God, he is ever awaiting God's requests.

In time I learned that Rev. and Mrs. Moon both maintained the strenuous sacrificial schedule that I have already mentioned, but that was a little different from the awareness I came to have of their internal selflessness that allows them to remain connected to God's holy presence and direction. Their selflessness frees them to continually put God and others first.

Since Rev. Moon has a naturally warm fatherly

presence, I unconsciously experienced the pure atmosphere surrounding him as an aspect of his fatherly nature, a kind of everyday ambience I enjoyed. Those of us who spent time with him could rest in that reliably pure spirit during the hours we were together.

Eventually I came to realize that God-centered selflessness and internal purity are virtues that by nature coexist in lives dedicated to God – they are two sides of the same coin. Rev. and Mrs. Moon selflessly put God first in their lives and embody God's refreshing absolute purity, which others can experience while working with them.

Even I have found that putting God first is a healing approach to life that opens up a much larger realm in which to pursue a marriage. Sunshine is more lifegiving and food tastes better when shared with God as well as my husband.

Rev. and Mrs. Moon have taught for years that we should master our physical bodies as they do, so our bodies don't dominate our souls. This is a daily process.

Everyone in our movement at the time I joined fasted for a week before being Blessed in marriage. It is a good experience to pray and fast because our bodies become less assertive, which frees our souls. Like most members, I have had various periods of physical self-denial, a few of which I have mentioned, that were dedicated to purposes that matter to me. My small sacrifices were not difficult because they were a genuine expression of my heart.

Still, it is only through unity with Rev. and Mrs. Moon themselves that I have experienced my spirit completely free and in control of my life.

Eternal Respect

When I met Rev. Moon, he was living in a positive, generous way that gave no hint of his ever having been tortured. He had left the physical suffering he had endured in his early manhood behind him, and he ignored later aches and pains.

Yet my own awareness of Rev. Moon's life when he was a prisoner in North Korea remains with me as an essential part of my understanding of who he is. When you know that someone has been willing to endure crushing amounts of suffering for your sake and the sake of others, as Rev. Moon has, it shapes your understanding of the meaning of life.

During Rev. Moon's years in North Korea, he forgave the unforgiveable, and he continued to wish good for the worst people. Rev. Moon perceives character honestly.

He is one with God's moral compass, which takes all of human nature into account – there are no rose-colored glasses. His agape love and concern for others are honestly based.

I have faith that in the spiritual world, Rev. Moon will not only uplift good people but also convert many of history's evildoers to God's side. He has the kind of rock-solid consistent goodness that is needed to overcome evil. He is so strong spiritually that the worst people can safely trust his concern for them not to waiver. He understands what people need and can show them what they can do to atone and heal.

I started my odyssey as an adult wondering about what it is in the human condition that allows for man's inhumanity to man. Encountering Rev. Moon, who could both understand and heal it was, and is, my good fortune beyond my ability to express it.

A life course undertaken in the sincere pursuit of God's providence, such as Rev. and Mrs. Moon's, may be long and arduous. I trust these two people, whether they are on earth or in the spiritual realm, to persevere until the world is transformed into God's dream.

In 2001, Rev. and Mrs. Moon stood on a history of providential accomplishment as a couple that made it possible for them to offer a crown of glory to God in a joyful ceremony. The Coronation of God honored and celebrated God reigning in heaven and on earth from the original position of the beloved Heavenly Parent of sinless sons and daughters. Rev. and Mrs. Moon are not only sinless themselves. Together they offer God the promise of a world filled with sinless children.

In 2003, Rev. and Mrs. Moon rededicated their own marriage. Because of their internal and external achievements, they can now stand before the world as the king and queen of peace and unity.

On January 13, 2013, another important milestone was reached. Cheon Il Guk or Foundation Day could be officially proclaimed. Rev. and Mrs. Moon had long looked forward to this day. It signified that their offering for the establishment of heaven on earth had been accepted by God. January 13 is the first day of 2013 according to the Heavenly Calendar, a lunar calendar recently adopted by our movement. Shortly before Foundation Day, Rev. Moon ascended to the spiritual world. Here on earth, Mrs. Moon presided over this significant ceremony representing their couple.

The dedication of the Cheon Won Gung, the cathedral on the Holy Ground of Cheongpyeong with its holy sanctuary, is a related milestone. This dedication in 2025 of a place for the world's people to pray and meet with God is a sanctified point on the earth from which God's presence can radiate to the world. It is a new beginning.

It feels as if the gates of Heaven are opening. We hope for additional celebrations of providential milestones. There is still much to be done. We look forward to the day that God's original creation will be fully realized and the people of the world will be able to rejoice together.

Messages for the Heart

Rev. and Mrs. Moon offer hope for the world. Because of Rev. and Mrs. Moon's birth, their marriage, and their sacrificial accomplishments, there is reason to believe that eventually our world can escape its present sorrows and become the land God originally intended.

Both Rev. Moon and his wife, as I know from experience, have lived in and make it possible for others to live in a high, pure spiritual atmosphere. It is the higher, freer world that I sensed was "out there somewhere" when I was young. When I have enjoyed the freedom of this spiritual realm, I have felt that all people could be totally free internally and naturally moral.

Rev. Moon has written an autobiography and Mrs. Moon a memoir. Rev. Moon's book is called, *As a Peace-Loving Global Citizen*. Mrs. Moon's book is titled, *Mother of Peace: And God Shall Wipe Away All Tears from Their Eyes*. Many other significant books covering the life and teachings of Rev. and Mrs. Moon are available in English.

I hope that readers have gained enough perspective from this account of my life to be skeptical of the misunderstandings, the gossip, and the outright lies about Rev. Moon's and his wife's life work and mission that have been and likely will continue to be invented. Change that improves the human condition is not always recognized at first.

Recently, we have come to call Mrs. Moon "Holy Mother Han" because that name highlights the connection between her sinless life and the religious history of the Korean people. Koreans use the word "Han" to designate their nation, its culture and distinctive qualities, and its stature as it respects Heaven.[9]

Holy Mother Han, by embracing this name, celebrates

---

9 In Korea, the word, "han" also refers to a feeling of sorrowful longing that is a part of Korean culture, a feeling of being as yet unfulfilled as the Koreans experience the imperfections and suffering of the world. There is a Chinese Han dynasty and a Chinese Han ethnic group, but these are not related to Korea.

Korea's dedication to God's providence over the centuries. Her name is helpful in expanding the world's awareness of Korea's consciousness of God and its religious roots.

The dedication to God of the Korean people, the Han, over the centuries made the births of Rev. and Mrs. Moon possible. Rev. Sun Myung Moon is from the Nampyeong Moon clan. Mrs. Hak Ja Han Moon is from the Cheongju Han clan. Among Korean families, these two lineages were specially prepared by God.

Koreans as a whole have an incredibly rare spiritual heritage. They are descendants of Noah's son Shem, the ancestor of Abraham, who is the father of faith for Jews, Christians, and Muslims. The Korean wing of Shem's family, guided by revelation, undertook the long journey that eventually brought them to the Korean peninsula. God planned for the world to have the security of heavenly culture planted in more than one location.

Had Jesus been widely revered in Israel when he was on earth, he could have married his own sinless bride who had been prepared for him at that time. Instead, he had to offer his life to atone for the failures and sins of others. By sacrificing his life, Jesus created the secondary providence of spiritual salvation for those who believe in him, as we know.

If John the Baptist, after testifying to the Lord Jesus, had become his chief disciple, Jesus' course could have been far different. John the Baptist was so respected in Israel that some even wondered if he was the Messiah. Other influential Israelites who were prepared to serve Jesus failed him as well.

When Jesus' disciples went out proclaiming to the people of Israel that Jesus was the Messiah, they were asked, "Where is Elijah?" In Malachi, the last book of the Old Testament, it is written that the prophet Elijah will come again before the Messiah: "Behold, I will send you Elijah the prophet before the coming of the great and terrible day of the Lord." (Malachi 4:5) The mission of Elijah is to prepare the way for the Messiah.

When the disciples asked Jesus, "Where is Elijah?" he told them that John the Baptist had been given the mission of Elijah. (Matthew 11: 14) We know that John the Baptist only testified to Jesus as the Messiah when he baptized him. Then John left Jesus. It is hard to imagine why John would depart if he was truly convinced that Jesus was the long-awaited Messiah. Had John been Jesus' chief disciple daily walking beside him, preparing his way, the people of Israel could have more easily followed the Lord Jesus.

Today, we are fortunate that Rev. and Mrs. Moon are surrounded by a cloud of witnesses. The world has been greatly enriched by the sinless marriage of the Lord of the Second Advent and God's holy daughter, and by the

Marriage Blessing they bring to the world. Each of these two amazing people, separately and together, contributes a depth of understanding of God that enhances life until it is truly fulfilling.

I hope that all the families of the world will soon be freed through the Marriage Blessing and will be able to move closer to God through the generations until God's original desire for human life, the kingdom of heaven on earth and in heaven, is realized, and God is totally free to dwell with every person ever born.

We dream of and imagine, even unconsciously, a world in which God and God's love are freely available to everyone. Many efforts have been made to improve life on earth, but the one that would make it possible for the others to come true would liberate God.

PART FOUR

Essays

Christianity's Gift of Freedom to America

As I mentioned earlier in the book, in 1976 at the time of America's bicentennial, Rev. Moon held two large rallies at which he spoke about the importance of the American founders' faith in God. I wanted to know more about their understanding of religious life and how it had impacted the development of the nation. When the bicentennial celebrations ended, I knew that I still needed a better grasp of the role of Christianity in America's founding so I continued to read about it.

Like most Americans, I was aware that early settlers had come here seeking religious freedom after having experienced religious persecution in Europe. I had assumed that the experience of religious persecution was the primary reason for the institutionalization of religious freedom here, and certainly it was important.

The English traditions of individual liberty and rights that early Americans carried with them from England also contributed, providing a supportive secular framework and environment within which to pursue religious freedom.

As I continued reading, though, soon I came to realize more clearly that the religious freedom the founders sought was anchored in their desire to protect the fundamental right of each individual to have the internal freedom to pursue a spiritually honest personal relationship with God.

Before I explore this thought, I would like to quote some of America's well-known founders talking about their faith. I am struck by the eloquence with which they expressed their deeply held religious convictions.

Thomas Jefferson said, "God who gave us life gave us liberty. Can the liberties of a nation be secure when we have removed a conviction that these liberties are the gift of God, that they are not to be violated but with his wrath? ... Almighty God hath created the mind free.... All men shall be free to profess, and by argument to maintain, their opinions in matters of religion."

John Adams stated: "The general principles on which the Fathers achieved independence were the general principles of Christianity." He famously asserted, "Our Constitution was made only for a moral and religious people. It is wholly inadequate to the government of any other. Morality and virtue are the foundation of our republic and necessary for a society to be free."

Noah Webster, who created the first American dictionary, asserted, "The moral principles and precepts found in the Scriptures ought to form the basis of all our civil constitutions and law. ... Christian religion ... is the source of all genuine freedom in government. ..."

Alexander Hamilton declared, "I have carefully examined the evidences of the Christian religion, and if I was sitting as a juror upon its authenticity, I would unhesitatingly give my verdict in its favor. I can prove its truth as clearly as any proposition ever submitted to the mind of man."

Patrick Henry, well known for having proclaimed, "Give me liberty or give me death," also asserted, "This is all the inheritance I give to my dear family. The religion of Christ will give them one which will make them rich indeed."

George Washington's Thanksgiving Proclamation of 1789 sets forth his firm faith in God: "Whereas it is the duty of all Nations to acknowledge the providence of Almighty God, to obey his will, to be grateful for his benefits, and humbly to implore his protection and favor ...

both Houses of Congress have ... requested me to recommend to the People of the United States a day of public thanksgiving and prayer to be observed by acknowledging with grateful hearts the many signal favors of Almighty God, especially by affording them an opportunity peaceably to establish a form of government for their safety and happiness..."

Affirmation of God's role in the creation of America is visible in the public speech of many other well-known early Americans and those who followed them including Abraham Lincoln. Though differences of opinion regarding the implementation of religious belief in public life abounded, freedom to express personal faith was not at issue.

The American Constitution comes from the founding fathers I have quoted and from others of their day who thought much like them. These founders believed that the virtues set forth in the Bible would nurture and preserve the democracy for which they were willing to risk their lives. Whatever misuses of Christianity may have occurred throughout human history, that was not the lens through which they viewed their faith. They were idealistic about the society they were creating.

The words of the Lord Jesus clearly establish the inherent value of each person. Each individual is most fundamentally God's son or daughter. Each life has been blessed by God to continue eternally. This broad understanding of the moral worth of each person provides a basis for a democratic society in which people are treated with respect and are entitled to dignity.

Christians are taught by their faith to love God and care for their neighbors. The Bible exhorts Christians to be morally responsible, to live with integrity, patience, honesty, kindness, and generosity. These teachings help people transcend self-centeredness and avoid the selfishness that is a common alternative to belief in God.

Christians are encouraged to examine their consciences and honestly face their faults. Since good and evil are mixed in each person, recognizing this reality motivates people to take an honest, kind, tolerant, moderate, and forgiving approach to others, which contributes to a healthy civil society.

We see in Jesus' Sermon on the Mount more socially valuable Christian virtues:

"Blessed are they which do hunger and thirst
   after righteousness…
"Blessed are the merciful…
"Blessed are the pure in heart…
"Blessed are the peacemakers…"

In early America, the Ten Commandments were

embraced as a foundation for the nation's legal system. The Ten Commandments teach that people should not kill or steal. They should be faithful to their husbands and wives. God is the ultimate moral judge. The Ten Commandments grounded the legal approach that the founders expected would protect their democracy by shaping a moral citizenry.

Beyond embracing the social virtues arising from Christianity, America's founders understood clearly that each person can communicate with God directly, that prayers are heard. They treasured and defended spiritual freedom because they believed it to be necessary for each person's authentic pursuit of his or her own essential relationship with God.

I have come to understand more fully that the freedom we take for granted in American life was embraced by America's founders importantly because they were, first and foremost, religious Christians who, as individuals, identified with their own and others' moral integrity and wanted to pursue personal spiritual relationships with God either alone or through worshipping with fellow believers.

They assumed that God, who has free will, has given each person free will. A living personal relationship with God is impossible without the believer freely wanting the relationship. The believer actively wishes to know God, to worship God, to honor God, to live together with God. The believer, of his or her own free will, wishes to give love to God.

This relationship cannot be coerced and remain the same. The founders understood that for them to fulfill their religious dreams, they needed to create a society that acknowledged and legally accepted that genuine relationships with God cannot and must not be coerced.

The institutionalization of religious freedom in America's founding also helped to establish peace in the larger society. Since religious freedom was genuinely embraced in America's founding, it was extended to faiths other than Christianity and to secular citizens. Striving for greater understanding of both religious and secular truth has prospered in this environment.

Since the founders wanted Christian integrity to thrive in a free atmosphere in America, they did not want America to be officially a Christian nation, one that forced office holders to be Christians. There was no religious test for federal office holders. There was to be no social pressure pushing them to conform to specific religious beliefs. Still, the early Americans had no qualms about expressing their own religious convictions in their public lives and assumed that others were free to do so. They pursued a delicate balance.

The First Amendment to the Constitution reads:

"Congress shall make no law respecting an establishment of religion..." This text was originally interpreted to mean that the federal government was prohibited from establishing a national church. This was its meaning for almost two centuries.

The Establishment Clause was re-interpreted in 1971 to pretty much exclude expressions of religion from public life. The case is Lemon vs. Kurtzman, and it resulted in the Lemon Test. The Lemon Test has three parts:

(1) the primary purpose of the assistance is secular,
(2) the assistance must neither promote nor inhibit religion, and
(3) there is no excessive entanglement between church and state.

This interpretation resulted in an abrupt diminution of the free expression of personal religious convictions outside of church services and private households. It was challenged in May of 2022 in Shurtleff v. Boston. The Lemon Test actually did not prevail, and the public expression of faith was ruled to be a reasonable and acceptable part of public life. There have been several other cases lately that were handled in this new way. Exactly where we are as a nation, I don't know. We haven't completely returned to the original interpretation nor are we strictly adhering to the Lemon Test.

How best to acknowledge the important Christian contribution to America's freedom as a nation and also affirm the personal freedom that the best of both religious and secular life require is still being worked out in American life. Personally, I have become more aware of how precious American Christianity with its embrace of religious integrity and religious freedom has been in shaping the life of the nation. I hope that Americans of all faiths and persuasions will continue to value this heritage.

Becoming a Better Teacher

Rev. Moon's thoughts about education led me to become a better teacher. Since I realize that not every reader is interested in classroom teaching, I'm sharing a positive teaching experience he inspired here in this essay at the end of the book.

Rev. Moon believes that the purpose of education is to know the heart of God in its many manifestations. This was the inspiration for a teaching method that I used with great success one summer soon after I had joined the movement when I volunteered to teach reading to African-American kids in a poverty-stricken neighborhood. Broken glass littered the ground of the recreation center where we met, but we had a quiet classroom. Any young person could come in so the students ranged from kindergarten to 9th grade.

My first thought after reading Rev. Moon's writing on education had been, "Who wants to educate each child more, God or me?" Surely God wishes to be the teacher. God knows each child's heart and mind. God loves each child unconditionally and knows what each child needs.

With this understanding, I hoped to invite God into the class so I based everything I did on prayer. I silently prayed deferring to God, "Heavenly Father, should I offer this book to Brianna now?" My prayers were usually answered. I might see that she was engrossed in the book she was reading and didn't need a new book at that moment. God's guidance made the classroom more comfortable and inviting. The classroom had a richer spiritual atmosphere than my earlier classroom in Harlem.

I was teaching using books borrowed from a nearby library. In the evening, I would go to the library and pray for each student as I searched for books that he or she might like. When I was teaching a lesson, I kept a prayerful heart. When a student was reading to me, I prayed silently for his or her success. This helped to create a bond between us because we were both investing our energy.

I should add that often the kids liked their books

enough that they read them more than once, read them to their friends, and drew pictures of scenes from their stories. There was almost no bad behavior. When there was a conflict, I typically stopped and prayed that the students could resolve the problem themselves. Usually this worked. Once in a while I had to ask them to please make peace.

I have some especially warm memories from this summer.

The first was when a twelve-year old boy discovered that he could read much better than he thought he could. I had gotten him *The Sugar Pear Tree* by Clyde Robert Bulla. In this story, a young boy, Lonnie, wins a pear tree, but, lacking a yard, he has no place to plant it. Soon his family even loses their home to eminent domain.

As I was reading this book to my student, he got so wrapped up in his urgent desire to find out what was going to happen that he started reading ahead. Would Lonnie ever have a home? Was Lonnie's pear tree going to die before he could plant it? My student was reading and then saying the words in a slightly altered way, expressing himself the way he naturally talked. As he made his way through the pages, he got more and more excited because he realized he could read so many of the words. His self-confidence soared. The other students were enthusiastic about his breakthrough and his excitement, and they spontaneously clapped for him. His mother was delighted, and so was I. I was grateful that he had felt free to follow his heart.

At the end of the summer, I invited my students to come with me to the public library. It was in a more affluent neighborhood. I didn't give instructions. I figured that since the kids had been in a reading program all summer, they should know how to act in a library. We met and walked over together.

There was a children's corner with books and games. The children picked out the ones they wanted. They were quiet and well behaved. They were the only African-Americans in the library. I sat nearby silently praying for them. When I got ready to go an hour later, I simply stood up. I didn't even say anything. All my students got up and put their books and games away. A couple students thanked the librarian on the way out. The librarian was surprised, and so was I.

The parents wrote good reviews at the end of the summer.

Because I had been a public-school teacher in the years after public prayer was banned from the public schools, and because I was teaching in a public rec center, I didn't pray aloud. I've wondered in retrospect if I could have, but since I didn't, I at least feel assured that even silent prayers inviting God into the classrooms so that there is a good spiritual atmosphere and there are comfortable personal relationships would be likely to improve academic success.

www.ingramcontent.com/pod-product-compliance
Lightning Source LLC
Chambersburg PA
CBHW061759070526
44586CB00023B/2627